About the author

Eamonn Ives is a Researcher at the Centre for Policy Studies, where he specialises in energy and environment policy. He is also a Research Adviser at The Entrepreneurs Network, and previously sat on the advisory panel of Climate Assembly UK.

Eamonn features frequently in the national media, and has written for The Times, The Telegraph, The Independent, CapX, CityAM, and ConservativeHome, among others.

About the Centre for Policy Studies

The Centre for Policy Studies was recently named by Conservative MPs polled by ComRes as the most influential think tank in Westminster. Its mission is to develop policies that widen enterprise, ownership and opportunity.

As an independent non-profit think tank, the CPS seeks likeminded individuals and companies to support its work, but retains editorial control of all of its output to ensure that it is rigorous, accurate and unbiased.

Founded in 1974 by Sir Keith Joseph and Margaret Thatcher, the CPS has a world-class track record in turning ideas into practical policy. As well as developing the bulk of the Thatcher reform agenda, it has been responsible for proposing the raising of the personal allowance, the Enterprise Allowance, the ISA, transferable pensions, synthetic phonics, free ports, and many other successful policy innovations.

Acknowledgements

Special thanks are given to EDF Energy for their generous support of this research. The author would also like to thank Robert Colvile for his careful editing of this report. A final acknowledgement is afforded to all of the individuals consulted with during the researching of the report for their insight, analysis, and evidence. Any errors of fact or judgment are the author's alone.

Contents

Executive summary

Britain's current framework for energy policy has delivered substantial successes.

The energy supply is reliable, and steadily decarbonising. The Government has also set out a sweeping vision for the future of energy, with the recent *Ten Point Plan for a Green Industrial Revolution*, promising a low-carbon wonderland in which there would be 'enough offshore wind to power every home', alongside advances in green hydrogen, nuclear energy, electric vehicles and carbon capture and storage.

> **❝ Multiple technological developments should help to facilitate the transition to a cleaner, cheaper, more intelligent energy system, in which the state can step back and permit the forces of market competition to truly take off.❞**

Yet it is fair to say that while the destination is set – reaching Net Zero by 2050 – the exact route map is far less clear. In particular, amid (or perhaps due to) the political and economic turbulence of the past several years, certain key decisions have been ducked for too long. This has bound the hands of the current Government, forcing it to intervene in the market to ensure that the country can keep the lights on while still progressing towards objectives such as Net Zero – and raising the risk that this will end up piling costs onto either consumers or taxpayers.

Multiple technological developments should help to facilitate the transition to a cleaner, cheaper, more intelligent energy system, in which the state can step back and permit the forces of market competition to truly take off. But for this transition to happen tomorrow, the Government needs to lay the foundations today – as well as solving pressing short-term problems in terms of energy supply.

This report therefore argues that:

- Britain needs an energy system which is fit for purpose – with adequate capacity to fulfil future energy demand in a way which is compatible with the Net Zero objective, but also minimises costs to consumers and businesses;

- Further decarbonisation of the energy system must be both economically prudent and practicably feasible. The exact pathway which offers the cheapest and most reliable route to decarbonisation cannot be known. Britain should not, therefore, gamble everything on speculative technological developments coming online as and when they are required. Instead, priority should be given to low-regrets options first;

- Amid this, some facts are known. Electricity demand will increase in the future – with some forecasting that demand could double to over 600 terawatt hours per annum by 2050. Meanwhile, Britain will lose significant quantities of zero-carbon power as its ageing nuclear fleet is decommissioned. Some of this baseload capacity loss will be met by Hinkley Point C, but without replacing more of it there is a sizeable chance that the UK will risk energy insecurity, and have to pivot back to fossil-fuelled power generation to keep the lights on. This could scupper any serious hope of meeting Net Zero;

- It is welcome that the Government has shown clear support for the continuation – and expansion – of the nuclear industry in the United Kingdom. This commitment is in keeping with advice from independent bodies, not least the Climate Change Committee, the National Infrastructure Commission, the Energy Systems Catapult, as well as many other energy analysts;

- We therefore agree that the Government should go beyond Hinkley Point C and support the further expansion of nuclear capacity, in order to bridge the gap to the low-carbon energy system of the future. In doing so, it is critical to facilitate future construction in a way which looks after the long-term interests of the general public, either as taxpayers or billpayers;

- One approach that has attracted interest is the regulated asset base (RAB) model. By allowing developers to charge energy consumers before generation commences, the RAB model can avoid the compounding of finance costs. This would bring down the overall cost of capital to developers compared to Hinkley Point C – and thus the total cost envelope to consumers, too;

- However, in a worst-case scenario, using the RAB model could add costs for either consumers or taxpayers. But the Government could take certain steps to avoid against this. For example, ex ante funding caps could be used, as well as penalties for late delivery of assets;

- Any decision should be subject to a rigorous value for money assessment, which simply considers how a decision will influence future energy costs alongside the UK's progression towards its climate objectives. Maximum project transparency should be guaranteed, to permit scrutiny from Parliamentarians and other interested parties;

- The construction of more nuclear generating capacity would provide a significant boost to Britain's energy security, in a way which is compatible with Net Zero. It would also have knock on benefits, such as ensuring there is a pipeline of skills and knowhow which will be requisite if the UK is to develop the next generation of nuclear technologies – namely small modular reactors (SMRs) and fusion reactors, both of which could aid the transition to a cheaper, greener energy system, but neither of which are yet ready for commercial deployment.

❝ It is welcome that the Government has shown clear support for the continuation – and expansion – of the nuclear industry in the United Kingdom.❞

As well as the above, fresh thinking is also needed to achieve a better energy system for the future. We argue that the Government should:

- Introduce a simplified and standardised price on carbon, to create a level playing field between energy generation methods, as well as stimulating markets in other green technologies and energy saving products to hasten progress towards Net Zero;

- Rationalise and streamline current decarbonisation policy, to ensure that regulations are proportionate, coherent, and necessary in getting to Net Zero in the most efficient and cost-effective fashion;

> **" The Government should deliver a better business environment for innovation, to promote research and development in green technologies which are required to decarbonise the economy."**

- Deliver a better business environment for innovation, to promote research and development in green technologies which are required to decarbonise the economy;

- Shift towards equivalent firm power capacity auctions – where Regional and National System Operators run capacity auctions which rate generators equally in accordance to their ability to supply firm power. This would normalise renewables in the energy system and further encourage innovation in renewable energy and storage in particular;

- Improve the regulatory landscape specific to the nuclear industry, in order to make sure the UK is not constructing any excessive barriers to this technology – especially in terms of future nuclear developments such as SMRs which are due to be commercialised in coming years.

I. Introduction

Every second of every minute, every hour of every day, we are critically reliant on a complex energy system which exists all around us.

It provides the electricity to power the computers in our offices, to illuminate the lights in our homes, and to keep the machines and equipment in our factories whirring away. It fills our vehicles' fuel tanks with petrol and diesel, allowing people and goods to be transported up and down the country. It feeds gas into our kitchens to cook our food, and into our boilers to keep us warm.

If the first responsibility of government is to safeguard its citizens, ensuring they have access to a secure and reliable energy system cannot come far behind – indeed, the two are intimately interlinked. Life as we know it would be impossible without the intricate energy system that has collectively and incrementally been built up.

Historically, the United Kingdom's energy system was almost entirely predicated upon the burning of fossil fuels. Today, 78.3% of the UK's primary energy is still derived from petroleum, gas, oil, and coal.[1,2] While such fuels provided the dense, concentrated energy necessary to break free from the shackles of grinding poverty, scientists have known for decades that their combustion comes at a grave environmental cost.[3,4]

> **❝ Since pre-industrial times, atmospheric concentrations of CO_2 have increased by 47% – and now stand at 415 parts per million. ❞**

When burnt, fossil fuels release carbon dioxide (CO_2) and other greenhouse gases into the atmosphere.[5] Since pre-industrial times, atmospheric concentrations of CO_2 have increased by 47% – and now stand at 415 parts per million.[6] This increase has caused the planet to heat up by around 1C, and rates of warming are increasing.[7]

For this reason more than any other, fossil fuels cannot be the bedrock of the UK's energy system going forward.

---

1 Department for Business, Energy and Industrial Strategy, *Digest of United Kingdom Energy Statistics 2020*. Link.

2 Primary energy refers to energy forms found in nature which have not been subject to any human conversion processes. For instance, gusts of wind captured by a turbine would be primary energy, while the electricity generated by it would be termed secondary energy.

3 For example, Guy Stewart Callendar, a British engineer and amateur climatologist, showed in 1938 how even relatively small concentrations of CO_2 in the atmosphere were warming the planet by compiling measurements of temperatures and CO_2 concentrations from the 19th Century.

4 Guy Stewart Callendar, *The artificial production of carbon dioxide and its influence on temperature*. Link.

5 Ibid.

6 NASA, *Carbon Dioxide*. Link.

7 Intergovernmental Panel on Climate Change, *Global warming of 1.5°C: An IPCC Special Report on the impacts of global warming of 1.5°C above pre-industrial levels and related global greenhouse gas emission pathways, in the context of strengthening the global response to the threat of climate change, sustainable development, and efforts to eradicate poverty*. Link.

To mitigate the country's ongoing contribution to climate change, in 2019 the Government set a legal target of reaching 'Net Zero' domestic greenhouse gas emissions by 2050.[8] This means that in fewer than three decades' time, no more greenhouse gases can be emitted in the UK than are removed from the atmosphere – for instance through natural sequestration, such as via trees, or other forms of removal, such as via direct air capture technologies.[9]

This policy was based on the Intergovernmental Panel on Climate Change's recommendation that global greenhouse gas emissions need to reach Net Zero by around mid-century if humanity is to have a reasonable chance of limiting global warming to 1.5C.[10] Following the UK's adoption of its Net Zero target, similar – or even more ambitious – goals have been set by other nations, as well as by many private companies, covering much of the global economy.[11]

Since legislating for Net Zero, the Government has also announced nearer-term climate objectives of its own – not least an aim to cut greenhouse gases by 68% on 1990 levels by 2030.[12] The Climate Change Committee (CCC) recently recommended a pathway to Net Zero would require a 78% cut to greenhouse gases on 1990 levels by 2035 – essentially bringing the original goal of the Climate Change Act 2008 forward by 15 years.[13] Within this, it envisages the electricity supply being entirely low-carbon by 2035 (with a carbon intensity of 10 grams of CO_2 per kilowatt hour of electricity produced), and virtually emissions-free by 2050 ($2gCO_2/kWh$).[14]

Achieving Net Zero will not be straightforward. To be more than just a noble aspiration, new long-term policy frameworks are required, as well as other measures necessary for developing and deploying the technologies that will ultimately bring greenhouse gases into an ecologically sustainable balance.

> ❝ To mitigate the country's ongoing contribution to climate change, in 2019 the Government set a legal target of reaching 'Net Zero' domestic greenhouse gas emissions by 2050. ❞

Successfully reaching both the 2030 and 2050 climate goals will require robust buy-in from the public – who understand the need for change, but will not tolerate unreasonable decrees from on high about how to order every facet of their lives, or huge increases in their energy bills, or having to contend with energy deficits on a regular basis. Ideally, therefore, the transition from a high-carbon economy to a low-carbon one should be as unnoticeable as possible.

To this end, the UK starts from an enviable position. Since 1990, it has managed to slash

---

8 Department for Business, Energy and Industrial Strategy, *UK becomes first major economy to pass net zero emissions law*. Link.

9 The Economist, *Climate policy needs negative carbon-dioxide emissions*. Link.

10 Intergovernmental Panel on Climate Change, *Global warming of 1.5°C: An IPCC Special Report on the impacts of global warming of 1.5°C above pre-industrial levels and related global greenhouse gas emission pathways, in the context of strengthening the global response to the threat of climate change, sustainable development, and efforts to eradicate poverty*. Link.

11 Energy and Climate Intelligence Unit, *Net zero: the scorecard*. Link.

12 Department for Business, Energy and Industrial Strategy and the Prime Minister's Office, 10 Downing Street, *UK sets ambitious new climate target ahead of UN Summit*. Link.

13 Climate Change Committee, *The Sixth Carbon Budget: The UK's Path to Net Zero*. Link.

14 Ibid.

its net domestic emissions from 793.8 million tonnes of carbon dioxide equivalent ($MtCO_2e$) to 451.5 $MtCO_2e$ in 2018 – a reduction of 43%.[15] Compared to other countries, the UK has been particularly successful – Germany, for instance, only cut its emissions by 36% over the same time frame,[16] and the USA actually increased its emissions by 3.7%.[17] In fact, of all the G20 nations, the UK boasts the fastest average annual rate of decarbonisation since the turn of the millennium.[18]

It should be noted that the UK has achieved this feat while both growing its economy (up 75% in the same timeframe),[19] and its population (up 16%).[20] Admittedly, progress is deceptive in some regards – the UK has, as pointed out in other Centre for Policy Studies work, offshored some manufacturing capacity and energy production,[21] and the figures do not account for international aviation and shipping.[22] But, overall, the country has a proud record on decarbonisation to date.

Yet there is still more to do. The equivalent of hundreds of millions of tonnes of CO_2 remains to be eradicated from the economy[23] – much of it from so-called hard-to-abate sectors, such as aviation, which as yet may only have nascent zero-emission solutions. Some sectors might not have solutions at all, and will require the scaling-up of greenhouse gas removal technologies to offset any emissions which are still being produced as 2050 approaches.

In the coming decades, therefore, major changes will be needed in the functioning of the UK economy in order to meet the Net Zero commitment. Decarbonising heat and transport will necessitate the generation of much more electricity – for instance to power electric heat pumps, or charge batteries in electric vehicles, or produce green hydrogen via electrolysis to be used in industrial processes, the transport system, and heating and energy storage.

> ❝ The equivalent of hundreds of millions of tonnes of CO_2 remains to be eradicated from the economy. ❞

All the while, this comes at a time when Britain is set to lose considerable amounts of existing 'firm' power – with coal- and fossil gas-fired power stations being retired, and long delays to the necessary decisions about whether to replace the UK's fleet of ageing nuclear reactors.[24,25] Failure to adequately prepare for this eventuality could risk domestic energy security, and the UK missing its climate objectives. This would damage the economy and the environment alike.

Fortunately, this is not a problem which has gone unnoticed. Politicians and experts are thinking hard about how the UK can ready

---

15 Department for Business, Energy and Industrial Strategy, *Final UK greenhouse gas emissions national statistics: 1990 to 2018*. Link.

16 Umwelt Bundesamt, *Indicator: Greenhouse gas emissions*. Link.

17 United States Environmental Protection Agency, *Greenhouse Gas Inventory Data Explorer*. Link.

18 PwC, *The Low Carbon Economy Index 2019*. Link.

19 World Bank, *GDP (current US$) – United Kingdom*. Link.

20 World Bank, *Population, total – United Kingdom*. Link.

21 Tony Lodge, *The Great Carbon Swindle: How the UK hides its emissions abroad*. Link.

22 Simon Evans, *The UK becomes first major economy to set net-zero climate goal*. Link.

23 Department for Business, Energy and Industrial Strategy, *Final UK greenhouse gas emissions national statistics: 1990 to 2018*. Link.

24 Firm power refers to electricity generation which can in theory be depended upon to effectively provide a set amount of power at any given moment.

25 Department for Business, Energy and Industrial Strategy, *BEIS 2018 Updated Energy & Emissions Projections*. Link.

its energy system for future challenges, without imposing unnecessarily high costs on businesses, consumers, and taxpayers. The recent Energy White Paper, eventually published in December 2020, provided the broad details of how the Government hopes to deliver a cleaner, cheaper energy system which locks in high-skilled, green-collar jobs.[26]

This report intends to contribute towards that discussion. Specifically, we begin by focusing on the state of the energy sector, and in particular the role of nuclear power.

> **" The recent Energy White Paper provided the broad details of how the Government hopes to deliver a cleaner, cheaper energy system which locks in high-skilled, green-collar jobs. "**

Our report then asks what an ideal future energy system would look like, and what this Government can do to make it a reality.

---

26 HM Government, *Powering our Net Zero Future*. Link.

II. UK climate and energy policy: past and present

As mentioned in the previous chapter, the UK has already experienced significant success in reducing greenhouse gas emissions.

This process has been driven, as Chart 1 shows, by the decarbonisation of the energy sector.[27]

Chart 1. Domestic greenhouse gas emissions (1990-2018)

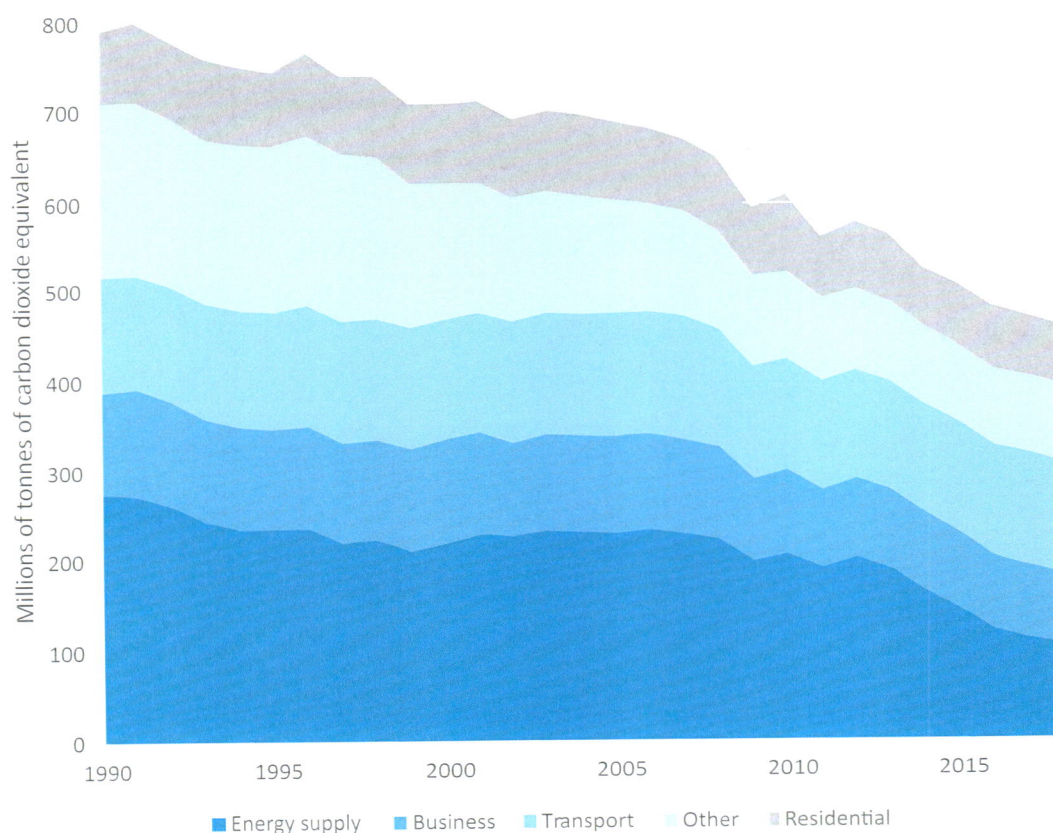

Source: Author's analysis of Department for Business, Energy and Industrial Strategy, *Final UK greenhouse gas emissions national statistics: 1990 to 2018*. Link.[28,29]

27 Hannah Ritchie and Max Roser, *CO₂ and Greenhouse Gas Emissions*. Link.

28 Excludes 'Land use, land use change and forestry' as this sector as a whole has always been a negative source of emissions over the time period referenced – sequestering 0.1 MtCO₂e in 1990 and 10.3 MtCO₂e in 2018.

29 Other includes emissions from Public, Waste management, Industrial processes and Agriculture.

For most of the period after 1990, the energy supply was the primary contributor to greenhouse gas emissions in the UK. Thirty years ago, it was responsible for around 35% of all emissions. Since 2016, however, transport has been the primary contributor of greenhouse gas emissions in the UK (accounting for 28% in 2018), with the energy supply now contributing 23%. In fact, since 1990, the energy supply has reduced its gross emissions by 173 $MtCO_2e$, or roughly 62% – and accounts for approximately half of all decarbonisation in the UK since 1990. (As mentioned above, a further 462 $MtCO_2e$ must still be cut or offset by 2050 if the UK is to successfully hit its Net Zero target.)[30]

There are a multitude of factors that explain this staggering reduction in emissions. The most obvious starting point is that Great Britain's electricity mix is now much cleaner than it once was.[31] Chart 2 shows how the 'carbon intensity' of Britain's electricity has fallen dramatically in recent years.

Chart 2. Carbon intensity of electricity (2009-2020)

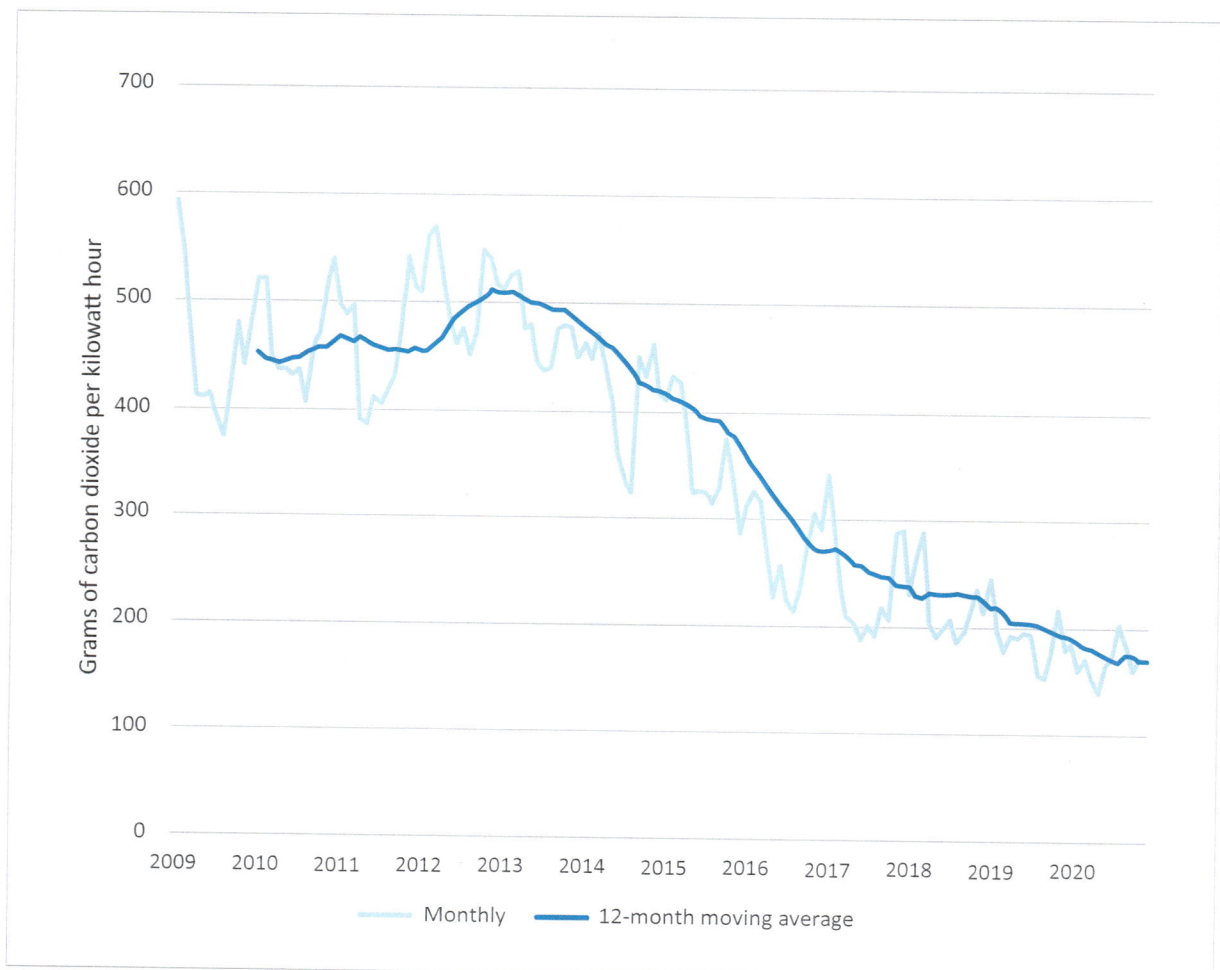

Source: Author's analysis of Drax, *Drax Electric Insights*. Link.

---

30 Department for Business, Energy and Industrial Strategy, *Final UK greenhouse gas emissions national statistics: 1990 to 2018*. Link.

31 Northern Ireland is part cf the Single Electricity Market with the Republic of Ireland, and our analysis is therefore limited to Great Britain, rather than the UK.

Having peaked in 2012 at 507gCO_2/kWh, average emissions for 2020 stood at just 169gCO_2/kWh. In other words, a reduction of nearly 67%.

Carbon intensity has fallen so rapidly because of changes in how electricity is generated. Chart 3 shows how the energy mix has shifted in recent years.

Chart 3. Electricity generation by fuel source (1998-2019)

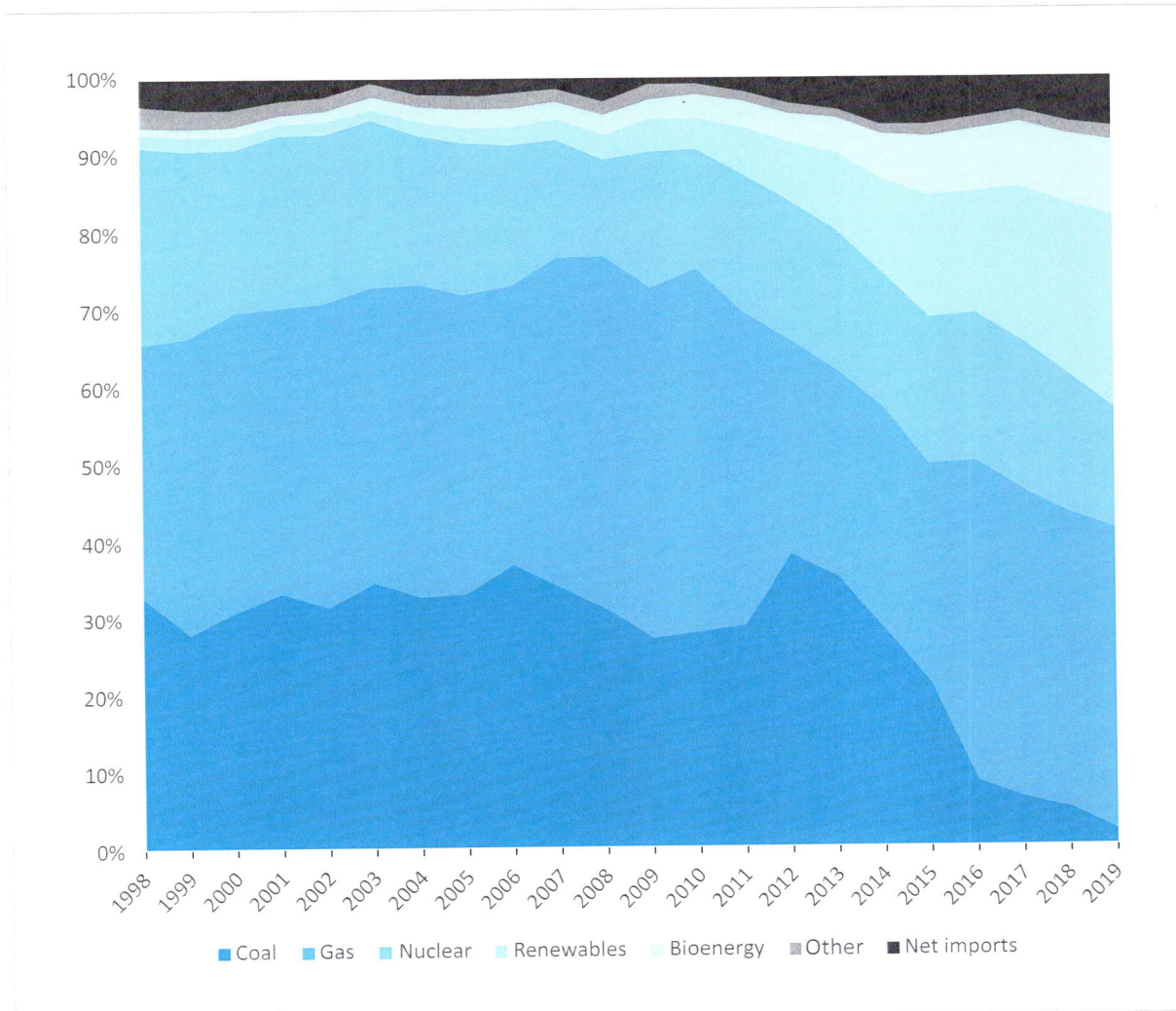

Source: Author's analysis of Department for Business, Energy and Industrial Strategy, *Energy Trends: UK electricity: Fuel Used in electricity generation and electricity supplied (ET 5.1 – quarterly).* Link.[32]

32 Renewables includes Wind and Solar plus Hydro (natural flow), Other includes Other fuels, Oil and Pumped storage (net supply).

A number of trends can be seen in these data, but two stand out as particularly noteworthy. First, coal-fired power generation has all but vanished from the electricity mix. Having supplied over 117 terawatt hours (TWh) of electricity in 1998 (33% of the total), coal provided just 6.54 TWh in 2019 (2% of the total).[33] Coal is set to be phased out from the energy system entirely by 2025, which may be brought forward to 2024 pending a public consultation – but at this rate, few will even notice.[34]

This reduction has had a remarkable impact on emissions, given just how polluting the combustion of coal is – producing around 990 tonnes of CO_2 per gigawatt hour (GWh) of electricity in 2019, compared to 370 tonnes of CO_2 per GWh for fossil gas.[35]

Second, the proportion of electricity generated by renewables has climbed markedly. In 1998, renewables provided a little under 6 TWh of electricity, of which only 0.88 TWh came from wind turbines and solar panels. Nowadays, nearly 83 TWh come from renewables, with wind and solar providing the overwhelming majority (77.27 TWh in 2019).

Accordingly, renewables now account for nearly a quarter of all the electricity generated in Great Britain, up from just 1.7% in 1998. In the coming years, solar and wind will grow their share even further, as a handful of big projects come online – such as Hornsea Two, an offshore wind farm consisting of 165 eight-megawatt (MW) turbines, which are able to power 1.3 million homes.[36] In October 2020, the Prime Minister set out his intention to have 40 gigawatts (GW) of installed offshore wind capacity by 2030, or enough to power every home.[37]

❝ Renewables now account for nearly a quarter of all the electricity generated in Great Britain, up from just 1.7% in 1998. ❞

Yet as well as the country producing cleaner electricity, it is also consuming a lot less of it to begin with. Chart 4 shows that electricity consumption actually peaked in 2005, at slightly over 349 TWh. In 2019, just under 295.5 TWh of electricity were consumed, a level not seen since 1994 – and nearly 15% lower than in 2005. This fall occurred as the UK's population grew by 10%, and as the economy by 13%.[38,39]

---

33 Department for Business, Energy and Industrial Strategy, *Energy Trends: UK electricity: Fuel Used in electricity generation and electricity supplied (ET 5.1 – quarterly).* Link.

34 Department for Business, Energy and Industrial Strategy, *Early phase out of unabated coal generation in Great Britain.* Link.

35 Department for Business, Energy and Industrial Strategy, *2019 UK greenhouse gas emissions, provisional figures.* Link.

36 Ørsted, *Hornsea Two: Powering well over 1.3 million homes with green electricity.* Link.

37 Prime Minister's Office, 10 Downing Street and the Department for Business, Energy and Industrial Strategy, *New plans to make UK world leader in green energy.* Link.

38 World Bank, *Population, total – United Kingdom.* Link.

39 World Bank, *GDP (current US$) – United Kingdom.* Link.

Chart 4. Electricity consumption in Great Britain (1986-2019)

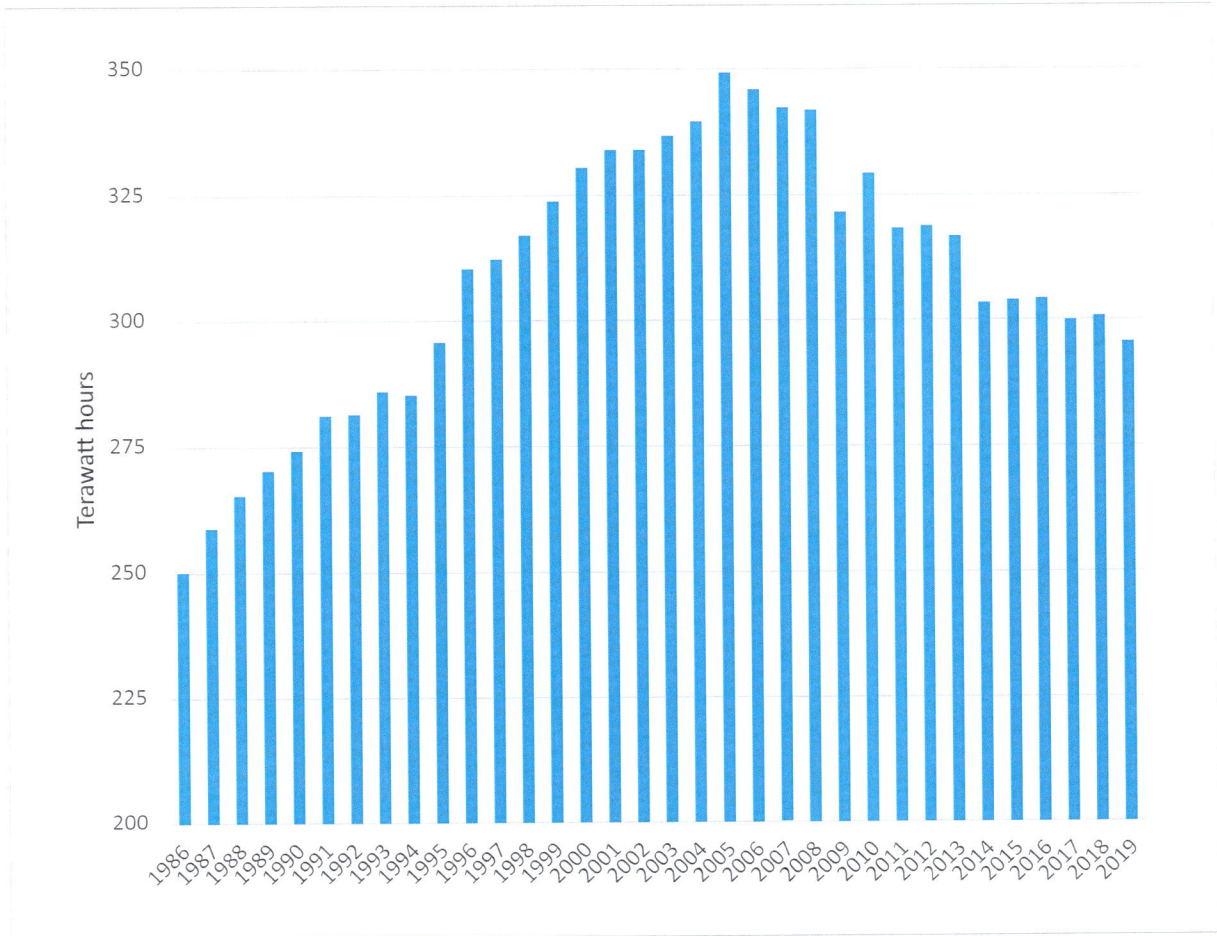

Source: Author's analysis of Department for Business, Energy and Industrial Strategy, *Historical electricity data: 1920 to 2019*. Link.

One of the primary drivers behind the reduction in electricity consumption is that everyday appliances have become increasingly efficient, and in some cases dramatically so. Chart 5 shows how the average amount of power needed for various household and office goods has tumbled since the 1980s.

Chart 5. Average electricity consumption of selected household goods (1980 = 100)

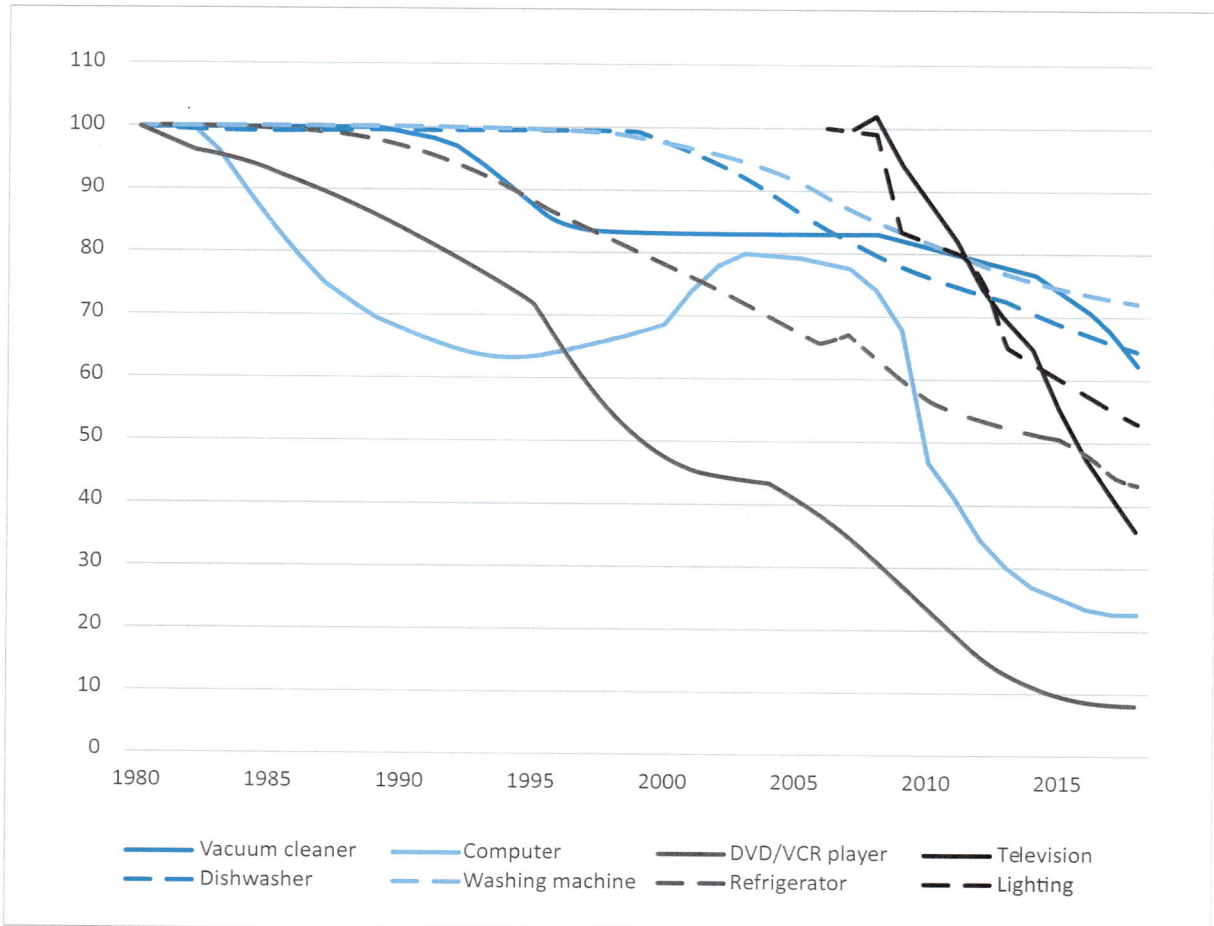

Source: Author's analysis of Department for Business, Energy and Industrial Strategy, *Energy Consumption in the UK (ECUK); Final Energy Consumption Tables.* Link.[40]

40 Lighting = 100 at 2006, and Television = 100 at 2007 due to data constraints.

In sum, Britain's electricity has become cleaner as fossil fuels have given way to renewables in generation, and ever less of it is being demanded in the first place thanks to energy efficiency gains.

With this in mind, it might be assumed that the energy supply's road to Net Zero should be relatively straightforward. On the current trajectory, with falling demand and cleaner supply, Britain will quite naturally see a situation whereby emissions shrink to virtually nothing.

To some extent, this will certainly happen. As old appliances, lightbulbs and other gadgets make way for new ones, they will doubtlessly consume less power than before. The electricity grid should only get cleaner as renewables continue to increase their share of generation, and dirty fuels such as oil and coal are consigned to the history books. Exciting developments in grid balancing technologies, and battery storage, will also mean energy can be consumed much more intelligently – minimising the need to produce as much overall.[41]

But significant challenges remain. Chief among these is ensuring that renewables really can help the electricity grid to make the transition to emissions-free power. Increasing their share from zero to almost a quarter is one thing, but increasing it from current levels to 60%, 70%, 80% or more is quite another.

Wind and solar produce variable electricity – because the amount they generate depends on whether the wind is blowing or sun is shining. After a certain point, the marginal cost of an additional share of variable electricity on the grid starts to increase overall costs, rather than seeing them fall, because of the need for expensive back-up generation in case of prolonged periods of lower output.

> " After a certain point, the marginal cost of an additional share of variable electricity on the grid starts to increase overall costs, rather than seeing them fall. "

One day in the future, a 100% renewable grid might well be viable – but for the near- to medium-term at least, renewables will almost certainly require other forms of generation to do the heavy lifting when they cannot.

Moreover, while electricity consumption has been falling in recent years, by all indications this will soon go into reverse as electric vehicles (EVs) and the electrification of other aspects of life become more ubiquitous. Indeed, according to the CCC, electricity demand could rise to around 677 TWh by 2050 in its 'Balanced pathway' scenario for decarbonisation.[42]

---

41 Amy Mount and Dustin Benton, *Getting more from less realising the potential of negawatts in the UK electricity market*. Link.

42 Climate Change Committee, *Sixth Carbon Budget – Dataset*. Link.

Chart 6. Forecasted electricity demand (2020-2050)

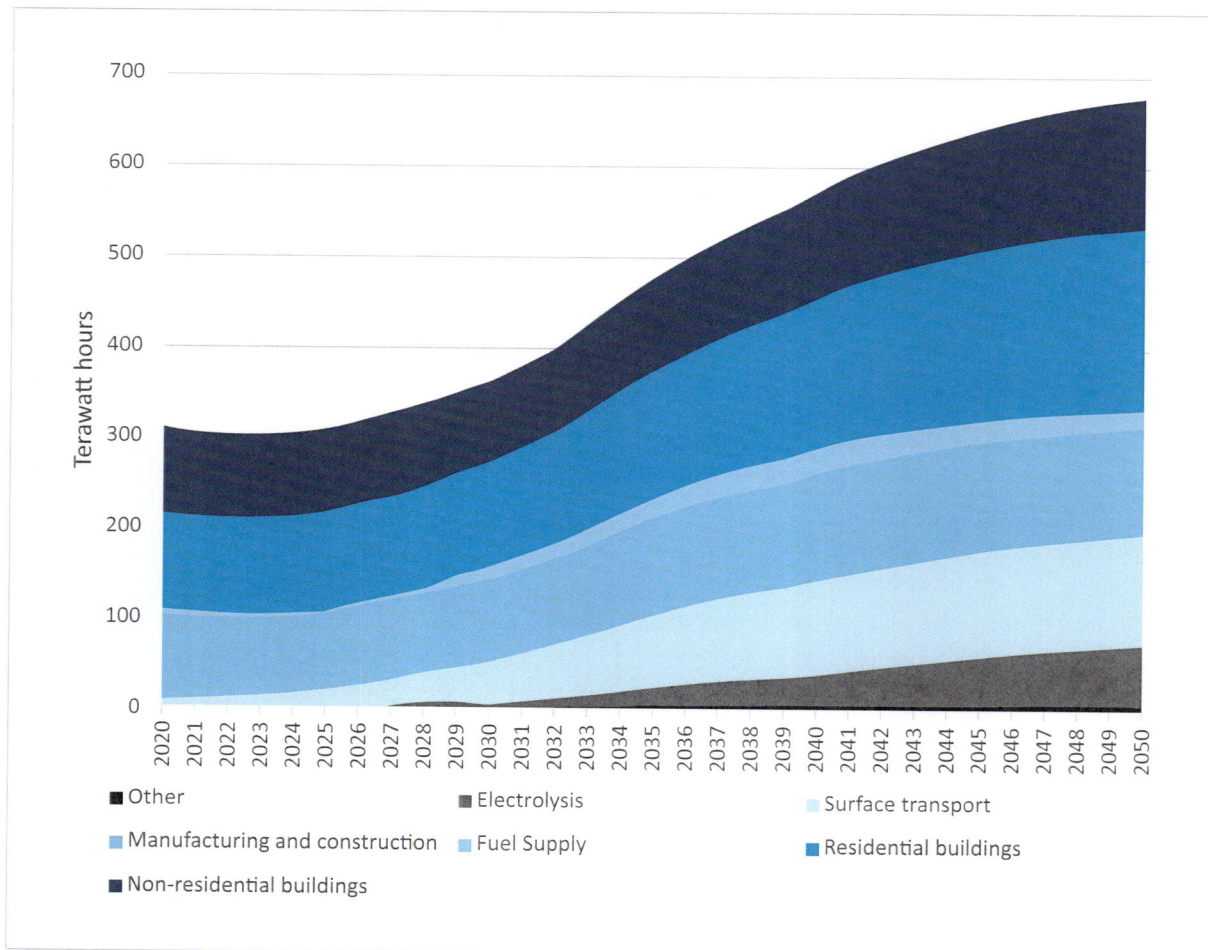

Source: Author's analysis of Climate Change Committee, *Sixth Carbon Budget – Dataset*, forecast is for CCC's Balanced pathway scenario made for its report on the Sixth Carbon Budget.

That is why this report is so necessary. We seek to examine how the UK can keep the lights on while remaining committed to Net Zero, in such a way which does not impose exorbitant costs on consumers – whether through higher bills or higher taxes.

III. UK climate and energy policy: looking to the future

So far, we have considered some of the broad changes in the climate and energy context over the past few decades.

In this chapter, we examine the changes which can be reasonably expected to occur in the next few decades, and what this could entail for policy in the energy sector.

Electricity consumption will increase as the economy electrifies

As already noted, electricity consumption in Great Britain peaked in 2005 – at just over 349 TWh.[43] Fast forward to 2019, and the country consumed a fraction over 295 TWh – a reduction of nearly 15%.[44] Yet, for a series of different reasons, this trend of falling consumption may not – in fact, almost certainly will not – continue.

Electrification is a primary enabler of decarbonisation.[45] The Government envisages vehicles with petrol- and diesel-powered engines being swapped for ones powered by batteries or hydrogen fuel cells. Gas boilers and stovetops will be replaced by electric heat pumps and induction hobs. Even certain industrial processes will be electrified – such as using electric arc furnaces for recycling steel, or plasma torches for cement production. Thus, as decarbonisation continues, electricity consumption will begin to rise once again.

There have been several attempts to model this. In the National Grid ESO's *Future Energy Scenarios 2020* (FES 2020), it provided multiple scenarios for how rapidly EVs will be adopted – as shown in Chart 7.[46] Its scenarios forecast that electricity consumption for road transport will increase from 1.4 TWh today to anywhere between 81 TWh and 87 TWh in 2050.

---

43 Department for Business, Energy and Industrial Strategy, *Historical electricity data: 1920 to 2019.* Link.

44 Ibid.

45 Electricity does, of course, create pollution if it is generated via the combustion of fossil fuels – but if done via harnessing wind and solar power, or through nuclear reactions, it can be regarded as zero-emission.

46 National Grid ESO, *Future Energy Scenarios: July 2020.* Link.

Chart 7. Forecasted number of EVs on the road (2020-2050)

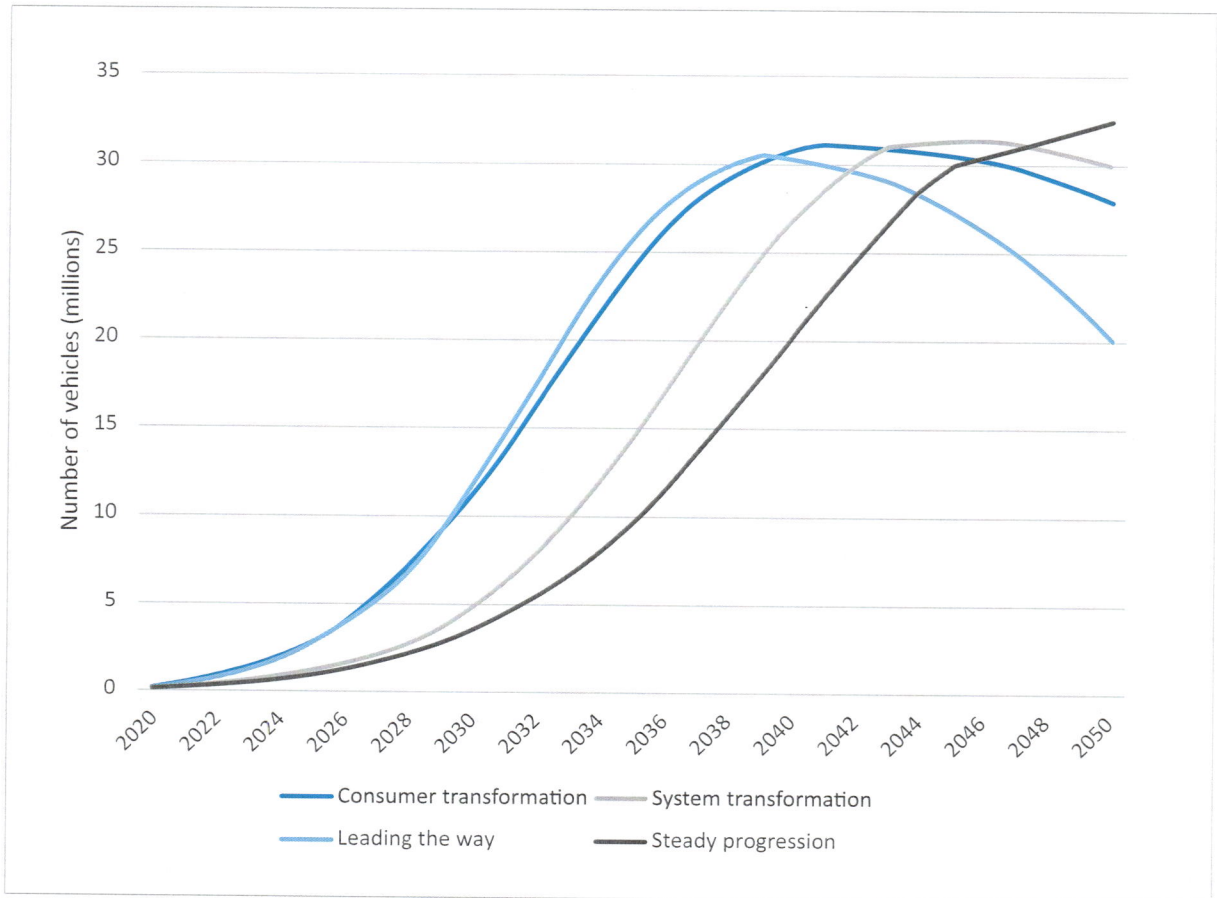

Source: Author's analysis of National Grid ESO, *Future Energy Scenarios: July 2020.* Link.

The same report also made predictions for how domestic heating will change between now and 2050. In three of its scenarios, it forecast the number of gas boilers shrinking from just over 24 million installed today, to fewer than 10,000 in 2050.[47] Heat pumps, on the other hand, are expected to rocket from around the 160,000 currently installed to perhaps 20 million or more 30 years hence.[48]

It should be noted that all of these estimates were made before certain recent important green announcements. In November 2020, for instance, the Government published its *Ten Point Plan for a Green Industrial Revolution*, which significantly accelerates its ambition to decarbonise the economy – for instance aiming to have 600,000 heat pumps installed every year by 2028, and bringing

47 Ibid.
48 Ibid.

forward the ban on the sale of new petrol- and diesel-powered cars to 2030.[49] A few weeks later, the CCC produced its report on the UK's Sixth Carbon Budget (2033-2037), which stated that a million heat pumps a year could be being installed by 2030, and that by 2035, 25 million purely battery-powered vehicles will be on the road.[50]

To be sure, electricity is not the only potential zero-emission energy vector which could decarbonise the UK's future economy. Hydrogen has long been touted as a way to decarbonise transport, heating, and industrial processes – indeed, the Centre for Policy Studies itself published a report, *Driving Change*, on this very topic in June 2020.[51] Again, in the *Ten Point Plan for a Green Industrial Revolution*, the Government stated an ambition to have 1 GW of hydrogen production capacity by 2025.[52] But if that hydrogen is to be compliant with the country's climate goals, it will need to be produced sustainably. This probably means via electrolysis – which would again necessitate a considerable increase in the generation of reliable, low-cost electricity.[53]

In sum, whichever pathway Britain takes towards decarbonisation, it is very likely to involve significant increases in electricity consumption – hence those forecasts that supply will need to more than double to 600 TWh a year by 2050.[54] The alternative is for Britain to abandon its climate objectives, put a cap on economic activity, or risk returning to an era of frequent blackouts and energy insecurity.

The composition of the UK's energy mix will continue to change

As shown above, the way in which electricity is generated in Great Britain has undergone an enormous amount of change in recent decades. Coal-fired power generation has almost vanished, while renewables have risen steadily. Going forward, no electricity whatsoever will come from coal, with solar and wind most likely making up the shortfall.

Yet even when coal is entirely removed from the grid, fossil gas will remain – providing a mostly dependable baseload of power, but also generating significant quantities of CO_2 in the process. While electricity produced by fossil gas peaked over a decade ago, if the UK is to abide by its climate ambitions, further reductions will need to be made.[55,56]

The Department for Business, Energy and Industrial Strategy (BEIS) publishes annual energy projections, which map many different variables under different conditions.[57] Chart 8 shows the forecast for electricity generation up to 2040 in the latest projection.

49 HM Government, *The Ten Point Plan for a Green Industrial Revolution: Building back better, supporting green jobs, and accelerating our path to net zero.* Link.

50 Climate Change Committee, *The Sixth Carbon Budget: The UK's Path to Net Zero.* Link.

51 Eamonn Ives, *Driving Change: How Hydrogen Can Fuel a Transport Revolution.* Link.

52 HM Government, *The Ten Point Plan for a Green Industrial Revolution: Building back better, supporting green jobs, and accelerating our path to net zero.* Link.

53 Ibid.

54 Committee on Climate Change, *Net Zero Technical report.* Link.

55 The CCC has a nominal target of electricity boasting a carbon intensity of less than 100gCO$_2$/KWh by 2030 in order to be on track to achieve Net Zero.

56 Committee on Climate Change, *Reducing UK emissions: 2019 Progress Report to Parliament.* Link.

57 Department for Business, Energy and Industrial Strategy, *Energy and emissions projections.* Link.

Chart 8. Projected electricity generation by source (2021-2040)

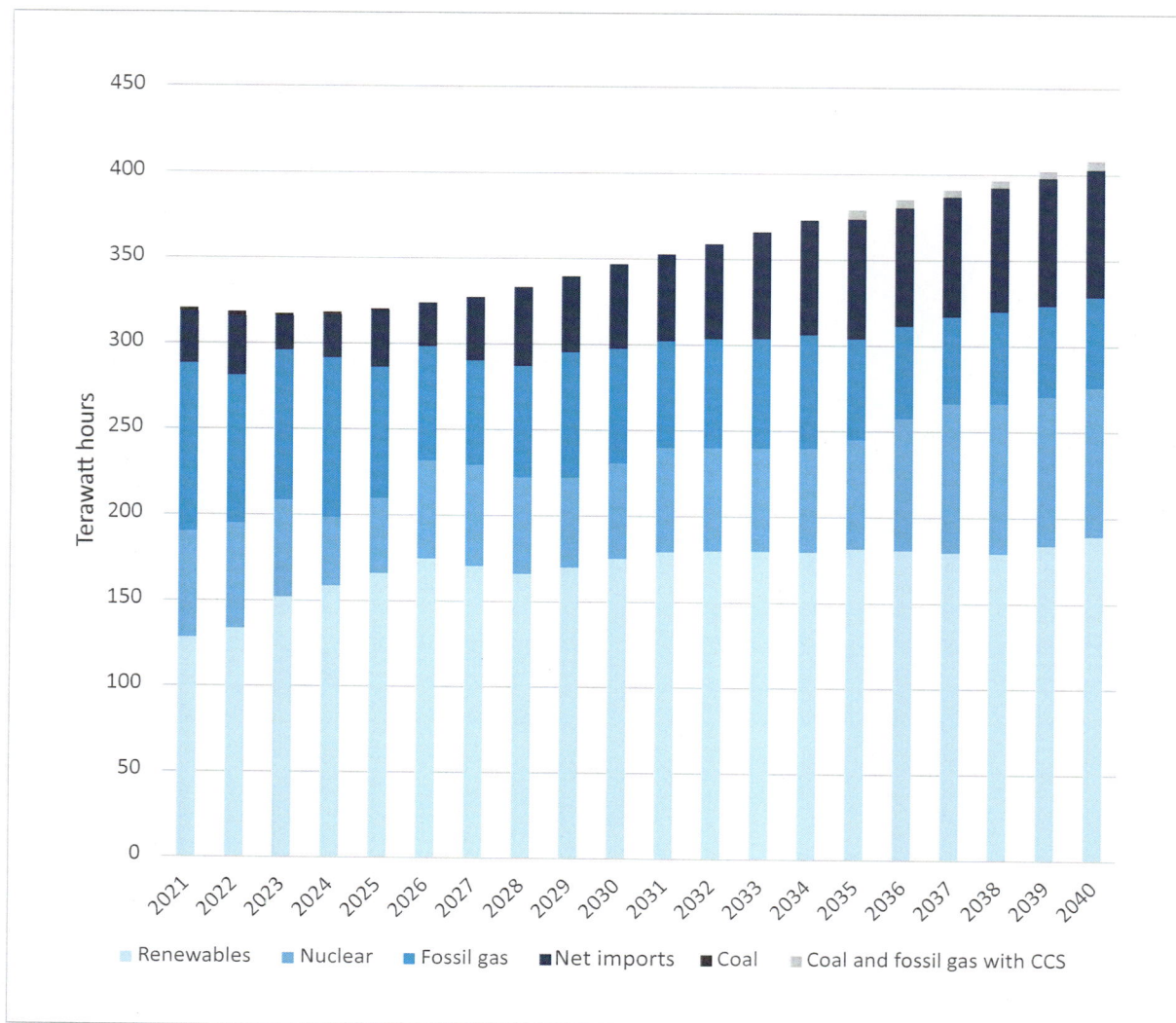

Legend: Renewables · Nuclear · Fossil gas · Net imports · Coal · Coal and fossil gas with CCS

Y-axis: Terawatt hours (0 to 450)
X-axis: 2021 to 2040

Source: Author's analysis of Department for Business, Energy and Industrial Strategy, *Updated Energy & Emissions Projections*. Link.[58]

BEIS project that by 2040, 46.5% of electricity will come from renewables, 21.2% from nuclear, 13.1% from fossil gas, 18.2% from imports, and 1.2% from coal and fossil gas with carbon capture and storage (CCS).

How the electricity mix will look after 2040 is inevitably less certain (and, indeed, the BEIS projections up until then still rely on speculation). Coal- and fossil gas-fired power stations which are equipped with CCS could start to make inroads (though this may depend on what scientific understanding emerges around fugitive emissions,[59] and advancement in CCS) and energy storage will almost undoubtedly increase. It is hardly unreasonable to assume that renewables will continue to occupy a larger share of total generation, while conventional fossil gas shrinks.

---

58 Excludes net storage, which ranges between -0.95 TWh and -1.27 TWh per annum for the time series.

59 Fugitive emissions are greenhouse gas emissions associated with the extraction, refinement, and distribution of fossil fuels. For example, gases might leak out from improperly sealed equipment, or pipes.

In previous Centre for Policy Studies work, we have pointed out the dangers in terms of energy security of relying increasingly on energy imported from Europe, given that times of highest demand in Britain are also likely to be times of high demand there. But a more fundamental question is whether renewables really can be depended upon to provide Britain with most of the energy it needs, when it needs it.

> ❝ Renewables are simply becoming much better, and are able to capture more wind or solar energy, which can be turned into electricity. ❞

There are some grounds for optimism that renewables will be up to the job. First, the cost of generating electricity through wind turbines and solar panels gets cheaper year after year in the UK – with the average levelised cost of electricity from offshore wind turbines down 26% since 2010, and down 83% for utility-scale solar photovoltaics (PV).[60] Renewables are simply becoming much better, and are able to capture more wind or solar energy, which can be turned into electricity.

Second, storage is also improving, and becoming more ubiquitous. As motorists steadily switch to EVs, for example, the country will have a fleet of batteries to utilise as storage for renewably produced electricity. Furthermore, as EVs become more advanced, technologies which facilitate vehicle to grid power transfer (commonly known as V2G) should allow for

much of the nation's transport system to not only act as a reservoir for excess electricity, but actively feed power to the grid when it is demanded, as if they were generators in their own right.[61]

Beyond batteries in cars, impressive strides forward are also being made in terms of the development of both battery units for homes, as well as much larger, grid-scale batteries – which can store renewably produced electricity when conditions are favourable, and release it to the grid when they are not.[62] Based on current technological learning trends, it would be foolish to bet against batteries continuing to improve to the point where they are a serious element of Britain's energy system.

Batteries are not the only way to store energy, however. Recently, a good deal of attention has been devoted to exploring the potential which hydrogen could have in helping to meet the energy needs of the future economy.[63] Zero-emission hydrogen can be produced by electrolysers running on entirely renewable electricity, and then stored for use at a later time. Though converting electricity into hydrogen only for it to be converted back into electricity is an inherently wasteful process (as energy is lost through conversion), electrolysers are becoming increasingly efficient, and as the renewables which power them continue to fall in cost, green hydrogen could yet play a significantly expanded role – particularly, as we have argued in previous Centre for Policy Studies work, in powering parts of the economy where electrification is prohibitively expensive or perhaps even physically impossible, such as heavy transport or seasonal storage.[64]

---

60 International Renewable Energy Agency, *Renewable Power Generation Costs in 2019*. Link.

61 National Grid ESO, *How smart charging can help unlock flexible capacity from EVs*. Link.

62 International Renewable Energy Agency, *Utility-scale batteries*. Link.

63 Eamonn Ives, *Driving Change: How Hydrogen Can Fuel a Transport Revolution*. Link.

64 Ibid.

Another method of energy storage, and one which is already widely proven and in use around the world, is pumped hydro storage. Here, water is first pumped from a lower reservoir into a higher reservoir when excess renewable electricity is being produced, and then released through a turbine when there is demand for electricity which is being unmet by renewables. The UK currently has 2,744 MW of pumped hydro storage,[65] which since the year 2000 has averaged 3 TWh of electricity generation a year.[66] According to RenewableUK, a trade association for renewable energy, there is potential to significantly increase pumped hydro in the UK in order to hit the Net Zero target.[67]

In other words, as renewables get cheaper and energy storage technologies get better, one can be quite confident that renewables will comfortably be able to provide an increasing share of total electricity demand.

Yet providing an increasing share does not equate to meeting all of the Britian's electricity needs. One of the reasons which makes achieving this feat so challenging

for renewables is their perennial drawback: variability of output.

> **" According to RenewableUK, a trade association for renewable energy, there is potential to significantly increase pumped hydro in the UK in order to hit the Net Zero target. "**

Data for 2020 show just how variable their generation can be. Last year, renewables met just 20% or less of demand for electricity on no fewer than 87 separate days. On ten occasions, there were three consecutive days where solar and wind met only 20% or less of total demand, including one stretch of eight consecutive days in August, and another of seven consecutive days in November. In 2020, one could observe days where renewables met as little as 5% of daily electricity demands, as well as days where they met more than 13 times that – fulfilling over 65% of daily electricity demands.

---

65 Department for Business, Energy and Industrial Strategy, *Digest of United Kingdom Energy Statistics 2020*. Link.

66 Department for Business, Energy and Industrial Strategy, *Fuel used in electricity generation and electricity supplied.* Link.

67 RenewableUK, *Powering the Future: RenewableUK's Vision of the Transition.* Link.

Chart 9. Daily share of electricity demand met by wind and solar (2020)

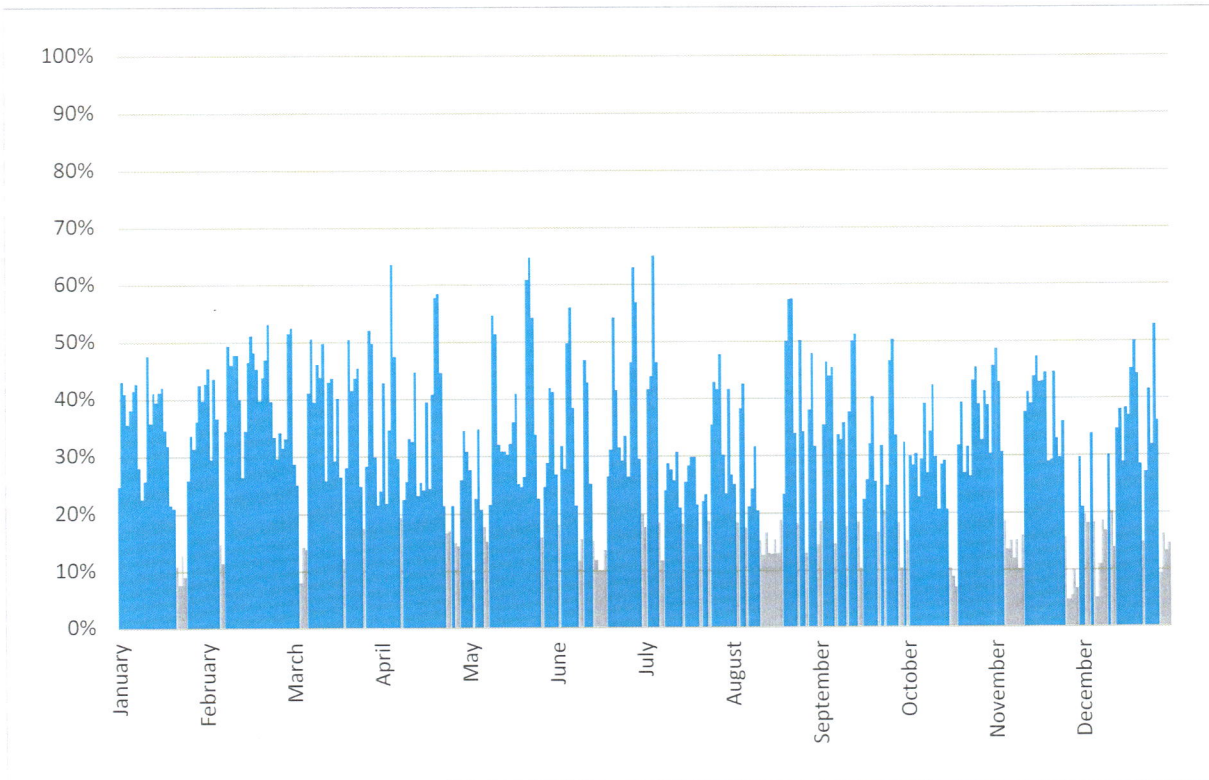

Source: Author's analysis of private data; grey bars indicate individual days where the share of electricity provided by wind and solar was equal to or less than 20% of overall daily demand.

Another downside to renewables relative to 'conventional' forms of power generation is that they cannot provide inertia to the electricity grid in the same way. Inertia refers to the kinetic energy which is stored in the spinning parts of the energy system – such as turbines – which rotate at the right frequency to balance supply and demand of electricity.[68] Having this inertia helps to moderate any sudden changes in system frequency, for instance if a generator stops producing electricity for whatever reason.

The above is not to denigrate renewable technologies. They are a critical part of Britain's energy system, and will make up an ever larger proportion of total generation in

years to come. But failure to recognise their current variability would be foolhardy.

Moreover, Britain needs renewables to be doing more than simply increasing the share of current electricity demand they fulfil. As noted, they need to so at a time when electricity demand is set to increase very significantly in gross terms – to facilitate the electrification of transport, industry, and heating.

If Britain is to function as normal going forward, it needs an energy system which can see it through cold, still, dark winter evenings, not just warm, breezy, sunny summer afternoons. In the following chapter, we will explore how this conundrum can be solved.

68 Paul Denholm et al., *Intertia and the Power Grid: A Guide Without the Spin.* Link.

IV. The nuclear question

As this paper has shown, renewables will be crucial to decarbonisation – but going for a 100% renewable energy scenario represents a considerable gamble, especially given that grid balancing and storage technologies are still relatively nascent.

The most pressing danger is that the solutions to renewables' inherent variability fail to materialise quickly enough, and Britain either has to live with constraints and interruptions to its energy supply – a political and economic no-no – or pivot back towards an energy mix of yesteryear, reliant on fossil-fuelled power plants to provide a dependable baseload of electricity, albeit at a great environmental cost. If this were to transpire, the UK would seriously risk reneging on its Net Zero target, imperilling the chances of limiting global warming to 1.5C or even 2C.

But there is also another big issue to consider: what to do when most of the UK's existing nuclear generation capacity is retired. By 2030, 14 of Britain's 15 existing nuclear reactors will have been shut down.[69] This translates to a loss of around 7.7 GW of generating capacity.[70]

As a power source, nuclear blends the best of renewables (zero-carbon generation) with the best of coal- or fossil gas-fired power stations (high dependability), as well as having some unique advantages of its own.

At a global scale, nuclear power prevented the generation of an estimated 63 gigatonnes of CO_2 between 1971 and 2018.[71] It is also incredibly safe relative to other forms of electricity generation – with research estimating that nuclear power results in just 0.01 deaths per TWh of energy produced, compared to 32.72 deaths per TWh of energy from brown coal, 2.821 deaths per TWh of energy from gas, and 0.035 deaths per TWh of energy produced from wind.[72,73]

> " At a global scale, nuclear power prevented the generation of an estimated 63 gigatonnes of CO_2 between 1971 and 2018. "

Beyond simply providing clean electricity, new nuclear could also play a significant role in decarbonising heat that is currently generated via fossil fuels – which accounts for around 37% of total UK CO_2 emissions.[74] As with all thermal power generation, nuclear power stations produce a considerable quantity of spare heat. It is possible to extract some of this

---

69 House of Commons Library, *New Nuclear Power*. Link.

70 Ibid.

71 International Energy Agency, *Nuclear Power in a Clean Energy System*. Link.

72 Anil Markandya and Paul Wilkinson, *Electricity generation and health*. Link.

73 Benjamin Sovacool et al., *Balancing safety with sustainability: assessing the risk of accidents for modern low-carbon energy systems*. Link.

74 Energy Systems Catapult, *Decarbonisation of Heat: Why It Needs Innovation*. Link.

heat for other uses, and many nuclear power stations around the world already do this. Higher grade heat of between 300-900C can be taken from steam before it enters the turbine generator in a nuclear power station (which can be used for process heat for industrial applications), and lower grade heat of between 100-200C can be taken from the turbine exhaust (which can be used for district heating).[75]

> ❝ New nuclear could also play a significant role in decarbonising heat that is currently generated via fossil fuels – which accounts for around 37% of total UK CO_2 emissions❞

Using the heat generated from nuclear reactors can also help in production of green hydrogen. Most green hydrogen is produced by electrolysing water. But electrolysing steam – created by boiling water with, for instance, nuclear heat – could increase the efficiency of electrolysis.[76] Research is also being carried out into thermochemical processes which use chemical cycles to split water molecules at high temperature into hydrogen and oxygen.[77] As hydrogen will play an enlarged role in the future economy, one might reason that the case for nuclear energy is significantly strengthened if the heat it produces can be exploited to aid the production of green hydrogen.

Another potentially useful application for nuclear heat is in direct air capture (DAC) for removing CO_2 from the atmosphere. Currently, there are two main technological approaches to DAC – one based on passing air through liquid chemical solutions, and another based on passing air over solid sorbent filters.[78] Each process binds CO_2 to the solution or sorbent, with heat then being used to release the CO_2. Once the CO_2 has been isolated, it can be permanently stored (for instance by injecting it into deep geological formations), [79] or used elsewhere in industry (for instance increasing agricultural yields or producing synthetic jet fuels).[80,81]

To be sure, nuclear power is not without its own drawbacks. Perhaps the most important is the radioactive waste it produces. As of 2019, the UK's stock of radioactive waste (ranging from 'very low level' to 'high level' wastes, and including waste from the medical, defence, and industrial sectors, as well as the power sector) stood at 132,590 cubic meters.[82] This would be enough to cover the pitch at Wembley, 30 meters deep, about twice over. In the grand scheme of things, this is a comparatively small amount – but obviously, the costs of containing and decontaminating such waste must be taken consideration when making decisions about future power generation.

The fundamental point, however, is that removing the UK's existing nuclear capacity without replacing it represents a considerable risk to meeting Net Zero, and to Britain's energy capacity and security. While it could well be possible to achieve

75 Royal Society, *Nuclear cogeneration: civil nuclear energy in a low-carbon future*. Link.

76 Shripad T. Revankar, *Nuclear Hydrogen Production*. Link.

77 Martin Roeb, Christos Agrafiotis and Christian Sattler, *Hydrogen production via thermochemical water splitting*. Link.

78 International Energy Association, *Direct Air Capture*. Link.

79 Valeria Perasso, *Turning carbon dioxide into rock – forever*. Link.

80 Simon Evans, *The Swiss company hoping to capture 1% of global CO_2 emissions by 2025*. Link.

81 Anna Holligan, *Jet fuel from thin air: Aviation's hope or hype?* Link.

82 Nuclear Decommissioning Authority, *Radioactive Waste Industry 2019 UK data*. Link.

Net Zero without any nuclear capacity beyond what is already installed, we believe that, as the Energy Systems Catapult have stated: 'Targeting [a system without any new nuclear] is risky (unlikely to get to Net Zero) and potentially expensive'.[83] This was backed up by the Government's own analysis in its recent Energy White Paper, which declared that additional nuclear capacity 'will be needed in a low-cost 2050 electricity system of very low emissions'.[84]

This nuclear policy headache has scarcely gone unnoticed. Yet in recent decades, depressingly little meaningful action has come as a result. However, in the last few years – and in particular in recent months[85,86] – the debate has significantly heated up.

History of nuclear power in Great Britain

In 1956, the world's first commercial nuclear power station opened in Sellafield, Cumbria.[87] Named Calder Hall, it had four Magnox reactors, and had a capacity of 196 MW.[88] It was designed to provide power for 20 years, although in the end was operational for over twice that – eventually closing in 2003.[89]

In the following 15 years, ten further Magnox power stations were opened across the UK – including Sizewell A, Hinkley Point A, and Bradwell.[90] The last Magnox power station – Wylfa – closed in 2015, having generated power for the previous 44 years.[91]

> **❝ In 1956, the world's first commercial nuclear power station opened in Sellafield, Cumbria. Named Calder Hall, it had four Magnox reactors, and had a capacity of 196 MW. ❞**

After the Magnox reactors came the advanced gas-cooled reactor (AGR) power stations.[92] Each of the seven AGRs built in Britain were constructed between 1976 and 1988, and, though beset by cost and time overruns during their construction,[93] all are still generating to this day (with installed capacities of between 1.06 GW and 1.25 GW).[94]

Britain's last new reactor, Sizewell B, was built in 1995.[95] Unlike the AGRs and Magnox power stations which went before it, Sizewell B uses a pressurised water reactor, with a capacity of roughly 1.2 GW.[96] Sizewell B was originally due to be closed by 2035, but EDF Energy, who run the plant, have stated a desire to extend its lifespan by a further 20 years.[97]

Eleven years after Sizewell B produced its first electricity, the then Prime Minister,

---

83 Energy Systems Catapult, *Nuclear for Net Zero*. Link.

84 HM Government, *Meeting the Energy Challenge: A White Paper on Nuclear Power*. Link.

85 HM Government, *Meeting the Energy Challenge: A White Paper on Nuclear Power*. Link.

86 HM Government, *The Ten Point Plan for a Green Industrial Revolution: Building back better, supporting green jobs, and accelerating our path to net zero*. Link.

87 Institution of Civil Engineers, *Calder Hall nuclear power station*. Link.

88 Ibid.

89 Ibid.

90 Department for Business, Energy and Industrial Strategy, *Energy Trends March 2019*. Link.

91 Ibid.

92 Ibid.

93 Robert Colvile, *Popular Capitalism*. Link.

94 Department for Business, Energy and Industrial Strategy, *Energy Trends March 2019*. Link.

95 EDF, *Sizewell B power station*. Link.

96 Ibid.

97 Nuclear Industry Association, *Nuclear Generation*. Link.

Tony Blair, announced in 2006 that the replacement of nuclear power stations was 'back on the agenda' – in order to cut greenhouse gas emissions, as well as to reduce reliance on imports of fossil gas from abroad.[98] Following this pronouncement, a Government paper was published, concluding that: 'New nuclear power stations would make a significant contribution to [the UK's] energy policy goals'.[99] It also indicated that it would be down to the private sector to propose, develop, construct, operate, maintain and finally decommission any new sites.[100]

> " In the recent Energy White Paper, the Government affirmed its intention to 'bring at least one further large-scale nuclear project to the point of Financial Investment Decision by the end of this Parliament. "

In early 2008, Gordon Brown's Government published a White Paper reaffirming that: 'New nuclear power stations should have a role to play in [the UK's] future energy mix'.[101]

Three years after that, in 2011, the Coalition Government issued a National Policy Statement which highlighted eight sites suitable for new nuclear power stations in England and Wales before the end of 2025: Bradwell; Hartlepool; Heysham; Hinkley Point; Oldbury; Sizewell; Sellafield; and Wylfa.[102]

However, despite new nuclear having been Government policy for more than a decade, the only nuclear project currently under construction in Britain is Hinkley Point C, which is being developed jointly by EDF and China General Nuclear Group (CGN). After years of legal wrangling and delays, it is now due to begin producing electricity in 2025, and will deliver 3.2 GW of power to the grid.[103] Hinkley Point C will provide some 7% of Britain's electricity needs based on estimates for 2025-2030[104] – but, per the Government analysis above, there are questions as to whether this will be sufficient to bolster security of supply as fossil-fuelled power stations are inevitably retired alongside the existing ageing nuclear reactors.

Status of new nuclear power stations for Britain

In the recent Energy White Paper, the Government affirmed its intention to 'bring at least one further large-scale nuclear project to the point of [Financial Investment Decision] by the end of this Parliament, subject to clear value for money for both consumers and taxpayers and all relevant approvals'. [105]

With regards to this ambition, the Government does not start with an entirely blank piece of paper. Plans already exist for other nuclear power stations to complement Hinkley Point C in replacing what will soon become lost generation capacity. EDF and CGN have proposed constructing two European pressurised

98 Tony Blair, *Speech at the CBI annual dinner (16 May 2006)*. Link.

99 HM Government, *The Energy Challenge*. Link.

100 Ibid.

101 HM Government, *Meeting the Energy Challenge: A White Paper on Nuclear Power*. Link.

102 Department of Energy and Climate Change, *National Policy Statement for Nuclear Power Generation (EN-6): Volume I of II*. Link.

103 Department for Business, Energy and Industrial Strategy, *Hinkley Point C*. Link.

104 UK Parliament, *Hinkley Point C Power Station: Question for Department for Business, Energy and Industrial Strategy: UIN HL2607, tabled on 26 October 2017*. Link.

105 HM Government, *Meeting the Energy Challenge: A White Paper on Nuclear Power*. Link.

reactors (EPRs) at Sizewell – Sizewell C – which, like Hinkley Point C, would produce 3.2 GW of electricity when up and running.[106] In addition, the two companies are looking to jointly develop a site at Bradwell in Essex – Bradwell B – with two Hualong One reactors, generating a combined 2.2 GW of electricity.[107] (Though in the wake of the Huawei 5G decision, there will inevitably be political sensitivities around the use of a Chinese design for such a core part of the electricity network, as well as the involvement of a state-owned Chinese firm.)[108]

In 2009, a consortium of energy companies operating under the name of NuGeneration Ltd acquired a site near Sellafield in Cumbria to develop what would become known as Moorside.[109] In 2018, however, the future of the site was thrown into disarray, when Toshiba – by then the sole backer of NuGeneration Ltd – announced it was winding the project up.[110] Two years later, however, two consortia – one led by EDF, and one led by Rolls-Royce – expressed interest in developing nuclear reactors on the site.[111]

Beyond this, various plans have been mooted over recent years to develop a new nuclear site on land beside a now decommissioned nuclear power station at Wylfa, in north Wales. The site's current owner – Hitachi – withdrew from developing a 2.7 GW plant there in September 2020, after years of fluctuating interest.[112] However, less than two months later, it was reported that an American consortium was interested in developing the site – claiming it could do so on a similar timescale, and at a competitive price if a suitable funding model could be brokered.[113]

> **" The principal reason why new nuclear power development has stalled in Britain is simple – finance. "**

As this suggests, the principal reason why new nuclear power development has stalled in Britain is simple – finance. All major infrastructure projects are, almost by definition, expensive undertakings. Significant amounts of capital need to be raised ahead of time, and projects might not deliver returns to investors for many years after funding has been secured, given the lengthy timeframes involved in building, for instance, a nuclear reactor.

As a result, virtually all concerned believe that the only way for new nuclear power stations to be built in the UK is with some form of support from central government. Certainly, this was the consensus among everybody we spoke to during the research stage of this report.

The main funding model currently adopted by the Government for supporting low-carbon power in the UK is based on the idea of 'strike prices' and 'Contracts for

---

106 House of Commons Library, *New Nuclear Power*. Link.

107 EDF and CGN, *Bradwell B*. Link.

108 Department for Digital, Media, Culture and Sport and the National Cyber Security Centre, *Huawei to be removed from UK 5G networks by 2027*. Link.

109 World Nuclear News, *New nuclear for Sellafield*. Link.

110 Toshiba Corporation, *Toshiba to Take Steps to Wind-up NuGeneration, Withdraw from Nuclear Power Plant Construction Project in UK, and to Record of Loss on Valuation of Stocks of Subsidiaries and Affiliates (Non-consolidated)*. Link.

111 BBC News, *Moorside: Nuclear power schemes proposed for Cumbria site*. Link.

112 Jim Pickard and David Sheppard, *Hitachi preparing to pull out of nuclear project in blow to UK climate ambitions*. Link.

113 Jonathan Ford, *US consortium revives plan for Welsh nuclear power plant*. Link.

Difference' (CfDs). These work by the Government (through the Low Carbon Contracts Company) agreeing a set price – the strike price – with developers for electricity produced over a given number of years, which is guaranteed by a private law contract known as a CfD.[114] The strike price therefore ensures a consistent level of return for the developer. When the wholesale market price for electricity is below the strike price, the developer is awarded the difference between the two prices. This 'top up' is ultimately paid for by higher electricity bills for consumers. When the market price for electricity is above the strike price, the developer pays back the difference to the Government.

Figure 1 illustrates how strike prices work. In this example, a hypothetical strike price is agreed at £70/MWh (here, the grey line). When the wholesale electricity price (here, the blue line) is below that value, the generator is paid the difference up to the value of the strike price (here, the shaded grey area). When the wholesale electricity price is above the strike price, the generator pays back the difference between that and the strike price (here, the shaded dark blue area).

Figure 1. Strike prices

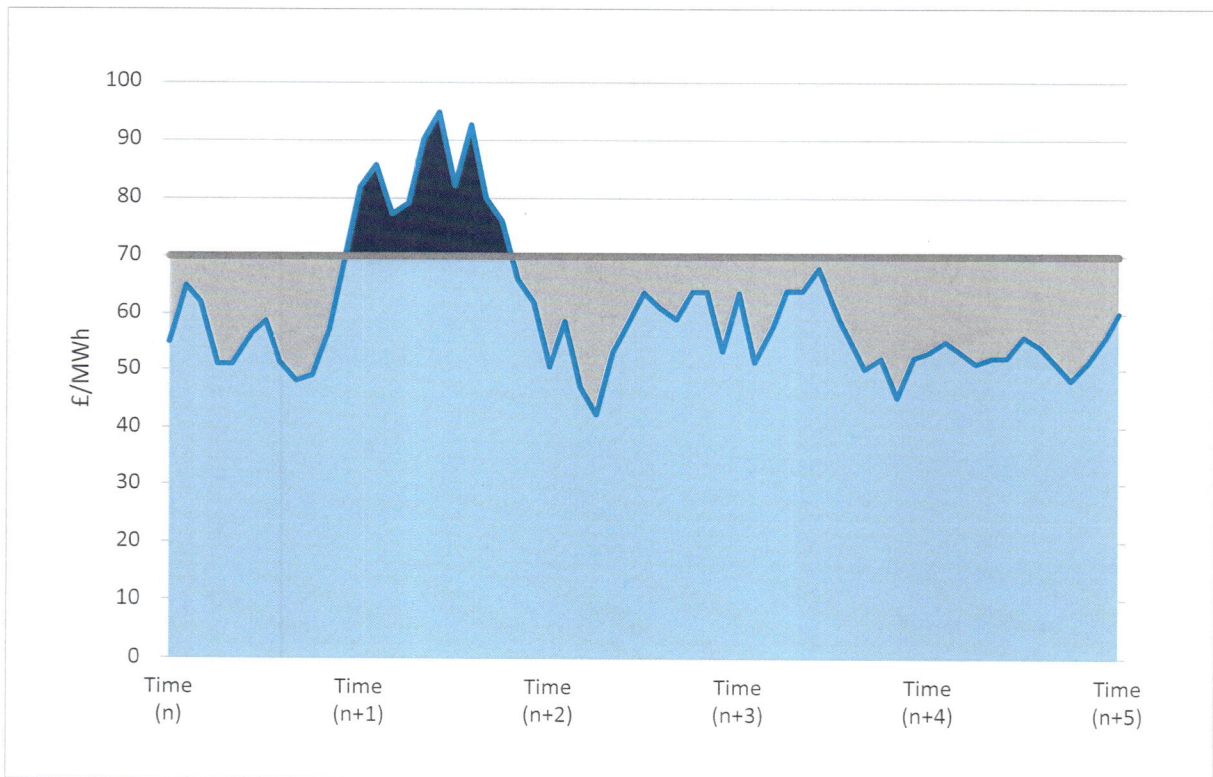

Source: Author's own – data shown are purely illustrative.

---

114   House of Commons Library, *Support for low carbon power.* Link.

Largely, CfDs are decided via 'allocation rounds', which are blind, reverse auctions. Before each allocation round, the Government sets a budget, and then sealed bids are submitted by developers of low-carbon technologies. The successful bids are selected sequentially in terms of lowest price to highest until the predetermined budget is exhausted. Allocation rounds therefore inject an element of competition between generators seeking to secure CfDs – which drives costs down.

> **❝ CfDs have been widely praised for their success in supporting renewables to transition from nascent to mature technologies.❞**

So far there have been three allocation rounds, and another will take place later this year.[115] Technologies which have benefited from CfDs include offshore wind, onshore wind, solar PV, and biomass, among others.[116] CfDs have been widely praised for their success in supporting renewables to transition from nascent to mature technologies, and for certain technologies' seemingly ever tumbling levelised costs of electricity generation. In the most recent allocation round, held in 2019, for instance, offshore wind projects secured a strike price of £39.65/MWh, a marked reduction on the strike prices of £150/MWh which were awarded in the first allocation round in 2015.[117,118]

CfDs can also be entered into bilaterally, outside of the allocation rounds. Indeed, this was how the Government proceeded with Hinkley Point C – which in 2016 secured an index-linked strike price of £92.50/MWh for 35 years, with the prospect of that falling to £89.50/MWh if Sizewell C is also developed.[119]

While the Hinkley Point C strike price compares favourably with the early CfDs for offshore wind, it is distinctly more expensive than the latest auction results – as well as involving a much longer-term commitment, given that most CfDs last for 15 years. In defence of the deal, comparing it with the CfDs struck for renewables is akin to comparing apples and oranges, as the two interact with the energy system in very different ways – and have other important differences in their characteristics. Nuclear can provide an extremely predictable baseload of power, while renewables will invariably be less reliable – and yet their costs do not necessarily reflect that. BEIS analysis shows, for instance, that while the estimated levelised cost of offshore wind in 2025 will be £54/MWh, its enhanced levelised cost – which takes into consideration variables such as integration costs – could be anywhere between £69/MWh to £85/MWh.[120]

Even so, in 2017, the National Audit Office produced a damning report in which it stated that the deal struck has 'locked consumers into a risky and expensive project with uncertain strategic and economic benefits'.[121] The then Energy Minister, Richard Harrington, subsequently said that this model was unlikely to ever be used again for funding new nuclear power stations.[122]

---

115   Department for Business, Energy and Industrial Strategy, *Contracts for Difference.* Link.

116   Ibid.

117   All strike prices are listed in 2012 prices.

118   Simon Evans, *Record-low price for UK offshore wind cheaper than existing gas plants by 2023.* Link.

119   House of Commons Library, *Support for low carbon power.* Link.

120   Department for Business, Energy and Industrial Strategy, *Electricity Generation Costs 2020.* Link.

121   National Audit Office, Hinkley Point C. Link.

122   Jillian Ambrose, *Government to rethink Hinkley Point funding model for future projects.* Link.

Nuclear's next top model? From CfD to RAB

If strike prices are out of the equation, what other methods of financing new nuclear are available? One which has garnered the support of the nuclear industry – and the interest of the Government – is known as the regulated asset base (RAB) model.[123]

> **" Using a RAB model to finance new nuclear power was first discussed in the House of Commons by the then Business Secretary, Greg Clark, in 2018. "**

Using a RAB model to finance new nuclear power was first discussed in the House of Commons by the then Business Secretary, Greg Clark, in 2018.[124] A year later, BEIS opened a public consultation on using the model for new nuclear, which closed in October 2019.[125] A summary of responses was then published alongside the recent Energy White Paper.[126] In this summary, the Government stated that: 'A RAB [model] in line with the high-level design principles set out in the consultation remains a credible basis for financing large-scale nuclear projects', and that: 'Government will continue to explore a range of financing options with developers, including [the RAB model]'.[127]

The RAB model works by an independent regulator establishing a price which a developer is subsequently allowed to levy on users in return for the provision of certain infrastructure.[128] In the case of a new nuclear plant this might, for instance, entail Ofgem setting the price, and an energy company building the power station charging energy suppliers accordingly. Energy suppliers would then in all likelihood pass on all or most of this additional charge to consumers through their electricity bills – as happens with CfDs. In other words, there is a basic similarity with strike prices in that the company that makes the investment will receive a guaranteed return – but the level is set by the regulator rather than the auction system.

The RAB model also differs from the approach of CfDs and strike prices in that the developer can start charging for infrastructure while the asset is under construction, as opposed to only receiving income for it once it is generating. In turn, this lowers investor risk and thus the cost of borrowing money, rendering the whole project a more attractive proposal for investors. As borrowing costs account for a significant portion of the overall cost of developing a new nuclear power station, the amount consumers are eventually on the hook for should in theory be lower too.[129]

The RAB model is already used widely in the UK to finance certain infrastructure projects, such as in the electricity, gas, and water networks. In 2016, it was also used to help secure funding for the Thames Tideway Tunnel (TTT) sewerage project.[130] By allowing Thames Water

---

123 World Nuclear Association, *Financing Nuclear Energy*. Link.

124 House of Commons Hansard, *Nuclear power: 04 June 2018: Volume 642*. Link.

125 Department for Business, Energy and Industrial Strategy, *RAB model for Nuclear: Consultation on a RAB model for new nuclear projects*. Link.

126 Department for Business, Energy and Industrial Strategy, *RAB model for Nuclear: Government response to the consultation on a RAB model for new nuclear projects*. Link.

127 Ibid.

128 Ibid.

129 Energy Technologies Institute, *The ETI Nuclear Cost Drivers Project: Summary Report*. Link.

bills to rise slightly to pay for the TTT, analysis estimates that the project will be approximately three times cheaper for consumers than initially envisaged.[131]

> ❝ If developers can start charging before plants are generating, the argument runs, consumers could end up sinking billions of pounds into infrastructure that might never be finished. ❞

Yet the RAB model is not without its critics. Some have questioned the wisdom of allowing extra charges to be added to bills long before consumers have anything to show for it.[132] This fear is only exacerbated by the fact that contemporary nuclear plants are highly complicated pieces of infrastructure, and the industry has not covered itself in glory in terms of delivering them on time or on budget. Projects in South Carolina and Georgia in the USA, and at Flamanville in France and Olkiluoto in Finland, have all exceeded initially expected costs or been scrapped altogether.[133] Globally, one paper from 2014 which studied 180 new nuclear plants found that 97% were delivered over-budget, with a mean cost escalation of 117%.[134]

If developers can start charging before plants are generating, the argument runs, consumers could end up sinking billions of pounds into infrastructure that might never be finished. At least with a CfD, where costs kick in only after construction is complete, billpayers are protected from this happening – in other words, even if costs escalate, consumers will have something to show for it, in the form of a finished plant which is able to generate power.

This criticism of the RAB model is definitely valid, and should be kept firmly in mind by policymakers when deciding how to proceed. That being said, there are reasons to think that the potential for the RAB to go quite so wrong in a manner detailed above will not necessarily transpire.

In the case of Sizewell C, for instance, it will be a virtual replica of Hinkley Point C. This should minimise the chances of cost overruns and delays. EDF and CGN will already have a reasonably accurate idea of capital and labour costs, and there will be a team with the required skills, equipment and knowledge that can transition to Sizewell C once Hinkley Point C is finished. Indeed, even within Hinkley Point C, the positive effects of prior learning are being demonstrated – with various construction stages being completed on the second reactor faster than they were on the first.[135] One of the reasons that the cost of Hinkley Point C was so high was that it involved rebuilding much of the UK nuclear industry from scratch, given the decades-long gap since the construction of Sizewell.[136] (Indeed, as discussed below, an argument in favour of approving new nuclear capacity is to ensure that the industry does not wither on the vine before small modular reactors (SMRs) and other new technologies are ready to come on stream.)

130 Cambridge Economic Policy Associates, *Background evidence: Review of the UK infrastructure financing market.* Link.
131 Ibid.
132 Citizens Advice, *Response to BEIS consultation on adopting a RAB model for new nuclear projects.* Link.
133 Michael Liebreich, *We Need To Talk About Nuclear Power.* Link.
134 Benjamin Sovacool et al., *Balancing safety with sustainability: assessing the risk of accidents for modern low-carbon energy systems.* Link.
135 Kirsty Gogan and Eric Ingersoll, *Drivers of Cost and Risk in Nuclear New Build Reflecting International Experience.* Link.
136 National Infrastructure Commission, *Net Zero: Opportunities for the power sector.* Link.

Admittedly, this logic would not apply to the same degree to other projects with more novel designs – the new plant at Wylfa being the obvious example. If the Government wishes to support the development of this power station, and other 'first of a kind' plans, there is more of a case against a RAB model, as it potentially leaves consumers even more exposed to the potential for costs to spiral and delays to occur. An evangelist of the RAB model might argue that if it means the cost of capital can be brought down dramatically, this financing packaging would still be better, even if it would be somewhat riskier.

However, it is possible to structure support for new nuclear investment in such a way as to potentially protect consumers against at least the most egregious examples of cost and time overruns. The BEIS consultation into the RAB model set out two different ways of doing this: ex post or ex ante.[137]

Under the ex post cost settlement approach, at set periods, the regulator overseeing the RAB would review the costs incurred by the project and decide on a discretionary basis as to whether they should be permitted to be passed on to consumers – depending on how and why they were incurred.

Under the ex ante approach, a target construction cost would be set for the project before work began. If costs exceeded this target, the excess would be split between investors and consumers in accordance to predetermined principles. This is the approach which was ultimately used for the TTT, and appears to be the favoured way forward for the Government if it does proceed with a RAB model for new nuclear.[138]

Clearly, there are arguments on all sides of the debate as to how new nuclear should or should not be supported in the UK. The RAB model offers the potential for lower overall costs, at the risk of (theoretically quite considerable) cost and time overruns. A CfD is less risky, if possibly more expensive in the round.

> **‘‘ Under the ex ante approach, a target construction cost would be set for the project before work began. ’’**

One should also keep in mind the political dynamics, too. Proponents of a small state might well baulk at the idea of the Government allotting tens of billions of pounds to private companies – either through consumer bills or taxpayer money, or upfront subsidies.

Beyond this, if the Government did proceed with a RAB model of funding new nuclear, other energy companies – such as those in the renewables sector – might reasonably question why they cannot also benefit from such privileged arrangements to bring down their costs. Or companies involved in the wider energy sector might lobby for similar support – such as those developing or installing energy efficiency upgrades, which would negate some of the need for the construction of additional power capacity. This would probably not be limited to the energy sector, either – plenty of other companies addressing all sorts of perceived social, economic or environmental ills could feasibly make the case that they too are worthy of support from the Government.

---

137 Department for Business, Energy and Industrial Strategy, *RAB model for Nuclear: Consultation on a RAB model for new nuclear projects*. Link.

138 Ibid.

The counter-argument is that a stable climate is a classic example of a public good – something non-excludable and non-rivalrous, which usually requires the state to intervene in order for it to be provided at the socially optimal level. So as with defence spending or vaccinations, even hard-nosed fiscal conservatives and advocates of free-market economics might concede that government intervention is appropriate without necessarily opening the door for further intervention in other aspects of the economy.

In summary, the Government has indicated that new nuclear capacity will be vital for keeping the lights on in a way which is compatible with delivering Net Zero – a view which we share.[139] New nuclear capacity can act as a bridge to a truly emissions-free energy system – providing a reliable stream of energy, and an insurance policy while renewables, storage, SMRs and other technologies are refined to the point where Britain can realistically begin to contemplate a grid powered exclusively, or at least overwhelmingly, by zero-carbon energy.[140]

As mentioned above, the development of at least one new nuclear site would also keep the door open – and skills and expertise in place – for other nuclear technologies.[141] If SMRs or fusion reactors are ever to be commercialised, the sector must be able to mobilise itself to plan, construct, and operate them – and beginning from a standing start, as the case was with Hinkley

Point C, would only make that endeavour more challenging and expensive.[142]

We are not alone in reaching this conclusion. Aside from the Government itself, a wide range of independent and respected bodies, such as the National Infrastructure Commission (NIC),[143] the Energy Systems Catapult,[144] and, to a lesser extent, the Climate Change Committee, are also supportive of the need for new nuclear power.[145] As the NIC put it:

> Cancelling the nuclear programme entirely risks a 'stop start' approach which is likely to be highly inefficient. Agreeing support for no more than one more nuclear plant before 2025 allows the UK to pursue a highly renewable mix without closing off the nuclear alternative.[146]

It is also worth pointing out that this conclusion was reached prior to the adoption of the 2050 Net Zero target, and indeed subsequent objectives, such as reducing greenhouse gas emissions by 68% on 1990 levels by 2030.[147] This was recognised in the Treasury's recent response to the National Infrastructure Assessment, which said that the step-up in ambition from an 80% reduction of greenhouse gases on 1990 levels to the 2050 Net Zero target 'means it is important to maintain options by pursuing additional large-scale nuclear projects'.[148]

---

139 HM Government, *Powering our Net Zero Future*. Link.

140 Ibid.

141 Eamonn Ives, *Nuclear reactors: is big beautiful?* Link.

142 Henry Fountain, *Compact Nuclear Fusion Reactor Is 'Very Likely to Work,' Studies Suggest*. Link.

143 Ibid.

144 Energy Systems Catapult, *Nuclear for Net Zero*. Link.

145 Committee on Climate Change. *Net Zero: The UK's contribution to stopping global warming*. Link.

146 National Infrastructure Commission, *Net Zero: Opportunities for the power sector*. Link.

147 Department for Business, Energy and Industrial Strategy and the Prime Minister's Office, 10 Downing Street, *UK sets ambitious new climate target ahead of UN Summit*. Link.

148 HM Treasury, *Response to the National Infrastructure Assessment*. Link.

Whether Britain should commit to developing new nuclear generating capacity or not, however, is only one part of the debate. The next is how – if at all – to support its financing.

The nuclear industry and most potential investors believe that the RAB model represents a viable mechanism of financing new nuclear capacity, especially relative to other arrangements, such as CfDs.[149] In its response to the consultation into the RAB model, the Government kept it firmly on the table as a potential financing option.[150] Yet, as we have shown, serious questions surround this approach – principally around whether developers really can abide by cost and time schedules.

These risks cannot be underplayed, and have the potential to leave either electricity consumers or taxpayers on the hook for considerable sums of money. So before agreeing to proceed with a RAB model for new nuclear development, the Government must consider in detail what it can do to mitigate these risks, whether through funding caps (set at a level which still ensures the RAB model is a more attractive means of financing new nuclear than the existing CfD framework), or some other mechanism.

To its credit, the consultation into the RAB model did begin to explore ways to protect consumer interests in the event it is used to finance a new nuclear power station.[151] We support the idea, for instance, that ex ante cost containment measures appear better than ex post ones. Setting out in advance how any potential pain sharing will be calculated only reduces risk – which is preferable for investors, developers, and, ultimately, consumers.

We also support the idea that subjecting a proposed project for RAB funding to a thorough and comprehensive value for money assessment is critical to ensuring that the best deal is struck for consumers. This would have to be carried out with maximum independence from the Government to avoid any further politicising of the process.

> **❝ The nuclear industry and most potential investors believe that the RAB model represents a viable mechanism of financing new nuclear capacity, especially relative to other arrangements, such as CfDs. ❞**

Moreover, its terms of reference – what it should take into account in terms of costs and benefits – should be limited strictly to how it will likely change the overall cost of the electricity system, and how it relates to the UK delivering on its Net Zero ambition without jeopardising security of supply. In BEIS's 2019 consultation on the RAB model, 'wider benefits' were alluded to being included in the value for money assessment – presumably referring to job creation and other potential economic stimulus effects it might have. Important as these are, we would urge the value for money assessment to stick firmly to the core question. As Citizens Advice said in its consultation response:

> [Job creation and economic stimulus] are not benefits that accrue to consumers as electricity bill payers, but rather that accrue to us as citizens in wider society. Paying for

---

149 Nuclear Industry Association, *BEIS consultation: Regulated Asset Base model for nuclear.* Link.

150 Department for Business, Energy and Industrial Strategy, *RAB model for Nuclear: Government response to the consultation on a RAB model for new nuclear projects.* Link.

151 Department for Business, Energy and Industrial Strategy, *RAB model for Nuclear: Consultation on a RAB model for new nuclear projects.* Link.

policies through bills rather than taxes is widely acknowledged to be regressive – those in the lowest seven income deciles would be better off if the cost of energy policies were moved from bills to taxes.[152] There are strong arguments for moving the cost of energy policies from bills to general taxation, and the case for asking electricity bill-payers to pay for benefits that have nothing whatsoever to do with the provision of electricity is particularly weak.[153]

> ❝ Transparency of spending must be paramount, as this would allow independent bodies – not least Members of Parliament and the Select Committees to which they belong – to scrutinise project delivery and safeguard consumers' interests. ❞

The Government has strongly indicated that a RAB model is its preferred way forward in terms of financing new nuclear power stations. In theory, it could do so at a cheaper cost to consumers than current arrangements – namely CfDs.[154] In practice, however, the performance of the nuclear industry in terms of delivering projects within budget and on time gives ample reason to be sceptical.

If the Government does press ahead with the RAB model for financing a further nuclear power station, it must ensure it is not locking consumers into a risky and potentially expensive arrangement. Mechanisms to isolate consumers from cost and time overruns – such as an ex ante cost settlement approach should be explored further, with low funding caps, and possibly penalties for late delivery of assets. Transparency of spending must be paramount, as this would allow independent bodies – not least Members of Parliament and the Select Committees to which they belong – to scrutinise project delivery and safeguard consumers' interests.

---

152   UK Energy Research Centre, *Funding a Low Carbon Energy System: a fairer approach?* Link.

153   Citizens Advice, *Response to BEIS consultation on adopting a RAB model for new nuclear projects.* Link.

154   Although it is perhaps again worth reiterating how virtually nobody believes another conventional-scale nuclear project could be financed through a CfD.

V. Shaping an energy system for 2050 and beyond

The previous section examined how the Government ought to proceed with regards to the financing of new nuclear capacity, in the context of current political and environmental realities.

These were, primarily, that Britain requires fresh investment in new nuclear power if it is to meet the substantial projected increase in electricity demand in a Net Zero-compliant manner, and that the Government will almost inevitably have to support this – but should do so in a way that limits the costs to consumers and taxpayers to what is strictly necessary.

> **❝ Despite having been privatised nearly three decades ago, energy has a long way to go before it can be treated as any other consumer good or service, operating under free-market competition. ❞**

In this chapter, however, we shall consider the kind of energy system and policy landscape Britain should be working towards outside the trappings of the present context.

As should be clear by now, the current energy sector is far from perfect. Owing to the legacy of decades of nationalisation perhaps more than anything else, the hands of successive administrations have been tightly bound, forcing them into suboptimal policy-making. Desires for genuine free-market competition in the energy system have also historically collided with technological constraints, as well as concerns such as energy security and limiting climate change.

Despite having been privatised nearly three decades ago, energy has a long way to go before it can be treated as any other consumer good or service, operating under free-market competition. Some might say that the characteristics of the energy system are such that a totally free market – or at least one which resembles the markets seen for typical consumer goods – can never be realised. Yet there is good reason to believe that arguments about natural monopolies, or negative externalities (most obviously the hundreds of millions of tonnes of greenhouse gases), will not hold quite as true in the future as they do now.

First of all, a large part of the perceived need for government involvement in the energy system is thanks to path dependency caused by previous decision making. But fresh decisions can also be made, and with long enough time horizons, businesses and individuals can be expected to adapt to new arrangements. In the recent Energy White Paper, the Government made its first forays into seeking to improve the fundamentals of how energy is generated, distributed, and consumed in the Britain.[155]

---

155 HM Government, *Powering our Net Zero Future*. Link.

Second, a suite of new technologies should soon come to the fore which will permit the realisation of a better energy system. Twinned with exciting ideas like 'open energy', they promise to help decentralise energy, make the whole system smarter, and should remove the need for a government to play quite such an enlarged role in how individuals purchase and consume their energy.[156]

Below, we detail five broad policy recommendations which the Government could adopt to foster a better energy system, which boosts energy abundance and security, while getting the UK closer to Net Zero more effectively, and doing so at less of a cost to consumers and taxpayers.

1) Simplify and standardise carbon pricing.

It is a well-worn adage that if you want less of something, you should tax it. Most conservatives intuitively appreciate the discouraging effect of taxes – whether applied to earnings, consumption or investment. The impacts of taxation are equally applicable to environmental pollution.

Already, the UK has a number of taxes aimed at tackling greenhouse gases.[157,158] These examples of carbon pricing are welcome – and insofar as the energy system is concerned, have helped to hasten decarbonisation. But the overall landscape of carbon prices in the UK is highly complex, unpredictable, and can often

work counterproductively.[159] As previous Centre for Policy Studies research has shown, they can also render businesses in the UK relatively less competitive by putting energy-intensive British firms at a disadvantage to their foreign counterparts which do not face carbon taxes in their own countries.[160]

> **❝It is a well-worn adage that if you want less of something, you should tax it.❞**

Advocates for free-market economics should be comfortable with the idea of carbon taxes.[161,162] Some might even demand that they exist, in order to create a true market containing as few market failures as possible.[163] Others might simply prefer them as the least-worst option to decarbonise the economy (in other words, a proper carbon tax would be preferable to the leftist tendency to favour a raft of mandates, regulations, subsidies, and other interventions, so long as it was brought in as a replacement for them rather than an addition).[164]

Either way, an appropriately levied carbon tax would account for the cost of the negative externalities which CO_2 emissions impose on third parties, and move the emissions of CO_2 towards a more socially optimal level – as per other Pigouvian taxes. Data suggest that the public also favour the broad principle of polluters having to bear responsibility for the damage they cause,

156 Sam Bowman and Eleanor Mack, *Open Energy: Using data to create a smarter, cheaper and fairer energy market.* Link.

157 House of Commons Library, *Carbon Price Floor (CPF) and price support mechanism.* Link.

158 Richard Howard, *Next steps for the Carbon Price Floor.* Link.

159 Energy Systems Catapult, *Innovating to Net Zero: UK Net Zero Report.* Link.

160 Tony Lodge, *The Great Carbon Swindle: How the UK hides its emissions abroad.* Link.

161 Here, we use carbon tax as a shorthand for a charge on the emission of all greenhouse gases on a CO_2 equivalised basis.

162 Eamonn Ives, *We need a carbon border tax to get Britain to net zero.* Link.

163 Kristian Niemietz, *Redefining the Poverty Debate.* Link.

164 Carsten Jung and Luke Murphy, *Transforming the economy after COVID-19: A clean, fair and resilient recovery.* Link.

and a carbon tax would be an elegant way of ensuring that happens.[165]

If a carbon tax were to be introduced in the UK, it would ideally cover as much of the economy as possible, so as to minimise economic distortion and ensure it is as effective as it can be in terms of promoting decarbonisation efforts. Achieving this in practice would see the carbon tax levied as far 'upstream' the economy as possible – meaning that it was paid as close as possible to the point at which carbon 'enters' the economy, such as when coal is mined from the ground, or oil or gases are piped from the depths and processed in refineries. Not only would this approach mean that as many potential sources of carbon as possible are taxed, it would also make the imposition of a carbon tax easier for both businesses and bureaucrats to manage, as only a handful of entities would be immediately subject to it.

> **❝ If a carbon tax were to be introduced in the UK, it would ideally cover as much of the economy as possible, so as to minimise economic distortion and ensure it is as effective as it can be in terms of promoting decarbonisation efforts. ❞**

Firms which are directly involved with bringing CO_2 into the economy – such as oil companies – would therefore be liable to pay the carbon tax. The tax incidence they shoulder themselves would, of course, be at their discretion. However, in all likelihood, much of it would be passed onto consumers in the goods they purchase as the products trickle 'downstream' in the economy.

It is through the alterations in the price mechanism this causes that the carbon tax would work its magic. An onus would be placed on individuals and private companies to appreciate the carbon consequences of all of their decisions. If they want to lower the costs of the things they buy, or the ways in which they operate, they now have a direct financial interest in avoiding CO_2, and therefore avoiding the carbon tax.

A future carbon tax should also make provisions for 'border adjustment'.[166,167] This means that when CO_2 intensive goods were imported into an economy, they would be liable to pay a fee in accordance with the UK carbon tax so as to avoid carbon leakage – whereby CO_2-intensive processes, such as electricity generation or steelmaking, are offshored to countries with less stringent standards on CO_2 emissions. It equally means that British exports should have the cost of their carbon tax rebated as they left the domestic economy, so as not to undermine the UK's competitiveness in exporting.

Finally, consideration would have to be given as to what happens to the revenues raised by a carbon tax. One way to ensure that a carbon tax – which is inherently regressive – is made progressive is to return money to citizens in the form of a carbon dividend. The exact form this takes should be consulted on, but, in theory, an equal share of money could be paid to all individuals in the UK, or perhaps households, based upon the amount the carbon tax raised in the proceeding interval. As lower-income individuals are typically

---

165 Climate Assembly UK, *The path to net zero: Climate Assembly UK: Full report.* Link.

166 Tony Lodge, *The Great Carbon Swindle: How the UK hides its emissions abroad.* Link.

167 Sam Lowe, *Should the UK introduce a border carbon adjustment mechanism?* Link.

responsible for the emission of less CO_2 than higher-income individuals, they are therefore less exposed to the carbon tax.[168] If designed properly, the poorest individuals could actually see their incomes rise as the result of a carbon tax, thus underpinning its progressivity.[169]

In December 2020, the Government opted in its Energy White Paper to establish a UK variant of the EU Emissions Trading System (ETS), which puts a cap on total CO_2 emissions from certain sectors, with that cap declining over time.[170] Firms are allocated tradable allowances to pollute up to a set amount, and are thus incentivised to reduce their emissions and trade their allowances with other firms who are unable to.

Yet while cap and trade systems are better than no policy at all, straightforward carbon taxes are superior policy instruments.[171] Carbon taxes are generally more predictable than cap and trade systems, which allow businesses to more accurately gauge what investments to make and when; carbon taxes are arguably more transparent and understandable, which builds salience among businesses and individuals; carbon taxes might be easier to administer, particularly if levied as far upstream in the economy as possible; and carbon taxes are typically less easy for special interest groups to manipulate.

The UK ETS commenced on January 1, 2021.[172] Given the political and economic volatility around the time of its introduction – principally the continued economic fallout from the Covid-19 pandemic and the possibility of leaving the Brexit transition period without a negotiated deal – it

perhaps made sense not to make any sweeping changes to carbon pricing, or worse, to risk abandoning one of the main forms of carbon pricing the economy had. But now that the UK ETS has carried over the framework of the EU ETS, the Government should seek to improve on it by shifting to a simplified and standardised carbon tax.

2) Rationalise and streamline decarbonisation policies.

The UK currently has a complex web of policies, schemes and directives aimed at reducing greenhouse gas emissions across all sectors of the economy. There are rules dictating how efficient certain appliances and vehicles must be, alongside mandates and subsidies promoting low-carbon energy sources. Such regulations exist to varying degrees across the breadth of the economy.

> **The UK currently has a complex web of policies, schemes and directives aimed at reducing greenhouse gas emissions across all sectors of the economy.**

Some degree of government intervention in the economy to prompt decarbonisation is currently necessary, because effectively decarbonising is a collective action problem and achieving a stable climate is a public good. Green regulations are one way of intervening, but by no means the only way. Moreover, they may not always be the most preferable way either – for reasons we shall explore later.

168 Ian Preston, Joshua Thumin et al., *Distribution of carbon emissions in the UK: Implications for domestic energy policy.* Link.

169 Citizens' Climate Lobby, *Household Impact Study: Financial Impact on Households of Carbon Fee and Dividend.* Link.

170 HM Government, *Powering our Net Zero Future.* Link.

171 Carbon Tax Centre, *Cap and trade.* Link.

172 Department for Business, Energy and Industrial Strategy, *Participating in the UK ETS.* Link.

Box 1 contains an overview of some of the main policies in the UK which seek to promote decarbonisation in net emitting sectors. These policies form the foundation of the UK's decarbonisation strategy. Without doubt, they have helped to reduce the quantity of greenhouse gases emitted by each sector. But whether or not they have facilitated this in the cheapest, fastest, or most efficient fashion is another question. Indeed, it is easy to point to certain schemes which have faltered – and in the worst instances may have actually served to increase emissions.

Box 1. Overview of decarbonisation policies in the UK per net emitting sector.			
Sector	**2018 greenhouse gas emissions**		**Sample policy interventions**
	Net emissions	**Percentage of total emissions**	
Transport	124.4 MtCO$_2$e	26.9%	- EURO standards for vehicle emissions - Fuel Duty and Vehicle Excise Duty - Grants for electric vehicles - Renewable Transport Fuels Obligation - 2035 ban on the sale of new petrol and diesel cars
Energy supply	104.9 MtCO$_2$e	22.7%	- Renewables Obligation - Feed-in Tariffs - Contracts for Difference - Carbon Price Floor
Business	79 MtCO$_2$e	17.1%	- Enhanced Capital Allowances for efficient goods - Non-Domestic Renewable Heat Incentive - Unabated coal powered electricity generation phase out by 2025 - Climate Change Levy
Residential	69.1 MtCO$_2$e	15%	- Energy Company Obligation - Green Homes Grant - Energy Performance Certificates - Domestic Renewable Heat Incentive - Gas boiler ban for new homes
Agriculture	45.4 MtCO$_2$e	9.8%	- Common Agricultural Policy Pillar II grants for decarbonisation - Funding streams for decarbonisation measures and best practice
Waste management	20.7 MtCO$_2$e	4.5%	- Landfill Tax - Recycling initiatives
Industrial processes	10.2 MtCO$_2$e	2.2%	- Climate Change Levy - R&D funding for CCS - Government-sector collaboration initiatives
Public	8 MtCO$_2$e	1.7%	- Non-Domestic Renewable Heat Incentive - Green procurement standards - Public Sector Decarbonisation Scheme

There is a rich body of literature on exactly why public policy-making to address societal issues does not always fulfil expectations. Public choice theorists have shown how policy-making can backfire, either through lobbying efforts from vested interests which leads to regulatory capture and rent-seeking, or simply socially suboptimal outcomes as a result of poor policy design.[173]

Consider, for instance, the 'cash for ash' scandal in Northern Ireland.[174] To boost the amount of heat generated via renewable sources, subsidies were awarded for renewable fuels under the Renewable Heat Incentive. But so generous were the subsidies that it actually made sense to overproduce heat – with stories abounding of individuals heating empty buildings simply to earn more subsidies.[175]

> **££ There is a rich body of literature on exactly why public policy-making to address societal issues does not always fulfil expectations. JJ**

Meanwhile, a Hayekian analysis would suggest that bureaucrats cannot possibly know exactly where or how emissions reductions can be most easily made, due to epistemological constraints.[176] For example, is it cheaper and more effective to replace fossil-fuelled energy capacity with renewables, or to invest in energy efficiency measures to lower energy demand overall? In the absence of market signals, policy objectives as complex as delivering on as Net Zero become all the more difficult due to the relative deficit of information.

The combined results of each of the above can make decarbonising more challenging and more expensive. Policies which artificially prop up what would otherwise be doomed industries pile extra costs on to bills, or hike up taxes. Funding which goes towards dead-end technologies ipso facto cannot go towards genuine climate solutions. The lack of comprehensiveness of the current policy landscape means that some sources of emissions go unaddressed, while others are more harshly punished than may be strictly necessary. Meanwhile, businesses face a nebulous, layered, and sometimes counterproductive framework of incentives – assuming that they are aware of what those incentives are in the first place. Many decarbonisation schemes have failed largely due to low uptake – which is perhaps not surprising when businesses and individuals have so many other things to contend with in their daily lives.[177]

The best way of cutting through this thicket, as we argue above, would be to replace the vast majority of these interventions with a simplified and standardised carbon tax would help drive down emissions. Set appropriately, it could be relied upon to do much of the heavy lifting in terms of wiping out the remaining emissions in the economy – in a way which responded far more promptly to market realities. Some regulations would still be needed, particularly to address niche emissions in hard-to-abate sectors. But the quid pro quo for the introduction of a carbon tax ought to be a comprehensive rationalisation of existing climate policies.

---

173 Eamonn Butler, *Public Choice – A primer*. Link.

174 Iain McDowell, *RHI Inquiry: Cash-for-ash – the story so far*. Link.

175 Ibid.

176 Mark Pennington, *Liberty, Markets, and Environmental Values: A Hayekian Defense of Free-Market Environmentalism*. Link.

177 Robert D. Marchand, S.C. Lenny Koh and Jonathan C. Morris, *Delivering energy efficiency and carbon reduction schemes in England: Lessons from Green Deal Pioneer Places*. Link.

Instead of hoping that Whitehall bureaucrats can reliably construct decarbonisation policies and schemes in the best possible way, power should be handed to businesses and individuals and allow the market to internalise the cost of emissions and steer behaviour via the price mechanism – just as happens so successfully in much of the rest of the economy.

3) Reward green R&D and create a pro-innovation business environment.

If taxes exist to correct for negative externalities, subsidies aim to promote positive externalities. Subsidies can come in many forms – such as direct grant payments from government to businesses and individuals, tax credits, or even regulations which dictate or steer private decision-making.

In recent decades, much innovation has come to fruition which is actively helping the UK and the rest of the world to decarbonise more quickly and at less of an expense.[178] Wind turbines are growing ever bigger, solar panels are becoming ever more efficient, and batteries in EVs are increasing their range.

This innovation hardly happens on its own. It requires time and resources to be devoted to research and development (R&D), to finesse existing technologies or design and install new ones entirely. R&D is not generally supplied by private markets to a socially optimal level, however, because it often has public goods characteristics. Principally, as the fruits of successful R&D are known to all – they can be seen and often copied by rival companies. Economists refer to this phenomenon as

the 'spillover effect'.[179] The incentive for firms to invest in R&D is thus diminished – why should a firm bother spending considerable sums on innovation when it can wait for another to do so first, then simply reproduce whatever it is they come up with?

Patents and other mechanisms can correct this to a certain degree, but even with these there is a general underinvestment in R&D. Furthermore, if a government designs too stringent a patent law regime, it limits the effect to which the benefits of innovation are dispersed. In the climate sector, this would deprive society of technologies which it will need if greenhouse gas emissions are to be cut without harming living standards or economic prosperity.

> ❝ In recent decades, much innovation has come to fruition which is actively helping the UK and the rest of the world to decarbonise more quickly and at less of an expense. ❞

To its credit, the current Government appears to understand this logic. In September 2019, the Ayrton Fund was created – a £1 billion fund to support British scientists to develop and test new technologies aimed at addressing climate change in developing countries.[180] A few months later, the Conservative Party won the 2019 general election on a manifesto which included a commitment to 'the fastest ever increase in domestic public R&D spending, including in basic science research', while also promising 'a new agency for high-risk, high-payoff

---

178 Eamonn Ives, *Green Entrepreneurship*. Link.

179 Sam Bowman and Stian Westlake, *Reviving Economic Thinking on the Right: A short plan for the UK*. Link.

180 Prime Minister's Office, 10 Downing Street, the Department for Business, Energy and Industrial Strategy and the Department for International Development, *British scientists to help tackle climate change through new £1 billion fund*. Link.

research'.[181] Clean energy was pinpointed as one of the key areas of focus.

At the 2020 Budget, plans were duly outlined to increase public R&D investment to £22 billion per year by 2024-25, taking public spending on R&D to 0.8% of GDP.[182] Changes to the Research and Development Expenditure Credit were made to leverage in as much private investment, too – increasing it from 12% to 13%, with a consultation announced on broadening its applicability.[183]

In July 2020, BEIS followed this up by publishing the *UK Research and Development Roadmap*.[184] This reiterated the positive steps the Government was taking with regards to innovation policy, but was full of other encouraging rhetoric, including ambitions to:

- Cut bureaucracy around public R&D funding;

- Convene an Innovation Expert Group to review and improve the whole innovation landscape;

- Establish an Office for Talent to proactively attract and retain the most talented individuals from around the globe;

- Embrace the idea that 'transformative research has a high chance of failure but can produce the greatest long-term rewards'.[185]

In both the Government's *Ten Point Plan for a Green Industrial Revolution* and the recent Energy White Paper, further funding pots were announced – such as £15 million for research into zero-emission aircraft, £20 million for a Clean Maritime Demonstration Programme, and £170 million for innovation on advanced modular nuclear reactors[186,187]

There is good evidence, therefore, to believe that the UK is heading firmly in the right direction with regards to R&D. Public budgets have been increased, and (crucially) the incentives for private firms to invest more in innovation have been strengthened. In light of this, the primary recommendation we make here is that the Government maintains its faith in the importance of R&D spending throughout

> **At the 2020 Budget, plans were duly outlined to increase public R&D investment to £22 billion per year by 2024-25, taking public spending on R&D to 0.8% of GDP.**

the lifetime of this Parliament, and rams the message home to civil servants, agencies and other bodies involved in tackling public problems.

Of course, encouraging R&D will take more than simply increasing funding. Perhaps the most important way in which to ensure

181 Conservative and Unionist Party, *Get Brexit Done: Unleash Britain's Potential.* Link.
182 HM Treasury, *Budget 2020.* Link.
183 Ibid.
184 Department for Business, Energy and Industrial Strategy, *UK Research and Development Roadmap.* Link.
185 Ibid.
186 HM Government, *The Ten Point Plan for a Green Industrial Revolution: Building back better, supporting green jobs, and accelerating our path to net zero.* Link.
187 HM Government, *Powering our Net Zero Future.* Link.

individuals and companies are developing the sorts of technologies needed to accelerate the UK's transition to a Net Zero economy is to have a sympathetic regulatory environment, in which there is a presumption in favour of businesses designing novel products or trying new ways of doing things.

> 66 Only by having a regulatory landscape which is conducive to allowing entrepreneurial ideas to come to the fore can the innovative, practical technologies be developed which will allow emissions of greenhouse gases to fall without curtailing human freedom or economic prosperity. 99

It is beyond the scope of this report to recommend exactly which regulations should be repealed or reformed if opportunities for R&D in Net Zero technologies are to be opened up. The key point being made here is rather that the Government should always be considering the impacts on businesses of the wider regulatory landscape in general. For instance, is it burdening firms by swamping them in bureaucracy? Is it creating regulatory moats which limit competition by locking in incumbents, and keeping dynamic would-be market entrants out? Does it adhere to Adam Thierer's description of 'permissionless innovation', which begs the question: 'Must the creators or new technologies seek the blessing of public officials before they develop and deploy their innovation?'[188]

Only by having a regulatory landscape which is conducive to allowing entrepreneurial ideas to come to the fore can the innovative, practical technologies

be developed which will allow emissions of greenhouse gases to fall without curtailing human freedom or economic prosperity.

4) Introduce equivalent firm power capacity auctions to create a fair future energy system.

One of the biggest developments in the energy system over the last 20 years or so has been the rise of renewables. In 1999, wind and solar provided 0.85 TWh of electricity, but in 2019, they provided 77.27 TWh (an increase of 8,991%).[189] In this time, the renewables themselves have undergone dramatic changes too – becoming more efficient, and a lot cheaper.[190]

Behind the headline costs per MWh of electricity generated by renewables, however, is a more complicated story – and one which becomes increasingly problematic as fossil-fuelled generation is necessarily retired from the grid.

Electricity generated by renewables is produced at effectively zero marginal cost. Most of the cost is borne when, for instance, the wind turbines or solar panels are installed, and then when they are decommissioned. Some is bound up in operation and maintenance (O&M) costs, and these are about as close to any marginal costs as one can get. This scenario is in stark contrast to, say, a combined-cycle gas turbine (CCGT) power station, which has relatively cheap capital costs, but requires expensive inputs to generate the electricity (largely the cost of the gas, plus taxes).

Yet, the perennial drawback of renewables, as we have seen, is their variability, which

---

188 Adam Thierer, *Permissionless Innovation: The Continuing Case for Comprehensive Technological Freedom.* Link.

189 Department for Business, Energy and Industrial Strategy, *Fuel used in electricity generation and electricity supplied.* Link.

190 International Renewable Energy Agency, *Renewable Power Generation Costs in 2019.* Link.

makes the cost of renewable electricity technically more expensive than it would otherwise be. In effect, the cost of electricity from a wind turbine or solar PV unit is essentially infinite when the skies are calm or the sun is not shining – because nothing at all is being produced. And when renewables are not feeding electricity into the grid, fossil-fuelled power stations are needed to ramp up supply to meet demand.

Renewables' relative unpredictability means that extra capacity needs to be built into the system, and be paid for – via higher consumer bills.[191]

Of course, over the coming years it will be possible to estimate and compensate for renewables' variability. We can be wholly confident, for instance, that solar PV units will not generate during the night, but reasonable estimates can be made as to how much they will generate during the day. Better weather forecasting means the predictability of wind turbine generation is improving. Increasingly intelligent and flexible energy systems are also better at incorporating renewables, as demand can be shifted up or down in response to fluctuations in generation.[192] Finally, storage options – whether that is batteries, green hydrogen, or something else entirely – should only continue to advance.

Yet, the fact remains that today's renewables are variable, and, at present, the electricity system somewhat turns a blind eye to that. For as long as we still have a reasonable proportion of fossil-fuelled generation on the grid, this is less of a problem – because coal- and gas-fired power stations can be ramped up to match energy demand. But as renewables occupy a larger share of total generation, however, current arrangements become altogether more precarious. Holding all other things equal, all it might take to risk energy insecurity in a world where renewables account for the majority of installed generation capacity would be a prolonged period of still, cloudy weather.

> **" Renewables' relative unpredictability means that extra capacity needs to be built into the system, and be paid for – via higher consumer bills."**

To guard against this possibility, the Government needs to look for alternatives. Fortunately, it has already done so. In 2017, BEIS commissioned Professor Sir Dieter Helm to review the cost of energy – which resulted in his *Cost of Energy Review* (more commonly known as the *Helm Review*).[193] In it, Helm laid out the idea of single equivalent firm power (EFP) capacity auctions, which would 'integrate the [Feed-in Tariffs] and low-carbon CfDs into the capacity markets'.[194,195] These EFP capacity auctions would entail the creation of a public National System Operator (NSO) and Regional System Operators (RSOs), which together would run auctions to ensure there is security of supply, so that when electricity is demanded, there is sufficient capacity to provide it.

---

191 Though it is worth noting that bills would be higher without any renewables on the grid, not least if Britain has a sufficient carbon tax to internalise the social costs of carbon associated with burning coal or gas, given how cheap renewables now are.

192 Eamonn Ives, *Green Entrepreneurship*. Link.

193 Dieter Helm, *Cost of Energy Review*. Link.

194 Ibid.

195 The Capacity Market commenced in 2018. It pays generators to be available to deliver power at times of system stress, such as when renewables are not generating significant amounts of electricity, or when demand is particularly high. Penalties result for generators which fail to deliver power when called upon.

EFP refers to the ability of a generator to produce a unit of power when called upon. In theory, no generator perfectly conforms to this ideal. Even what are termed baseload power stations are somewhat – even if only fractionally – unreliable at certain points in time. Coal, gas, and nuclear power stations are periodically taken offline for maintenance, or, in the worst instances, because of unforeseen faults during operation. That said, fossil-fuelled generation and nuclear are about as dependable as it gets – and would score highly in an EFP capacity auction.

At the other end of the spectrum, variable generators such as wind turbines and solar PV would fare less well. Though they produce electricity more predictably than many imagine, and should become more reliable still in coming years, renewables would be derated in an EFP capacity auction to reflect the fact that they will not always be able to provide power when called upon.

> ❝ EFP capacity auctions provide a competitive, market-based framework through which electricity is procured on a level playing field basis from an energy security point of view. ❞

EFP capacity auctions thus provide a competitive, market-based framework through which electricity is procured on a level playing field basis from an energy security point of view. They shift the focus squarely onto generators, and whether or not they can satisfy forecasted demand.

Prima facie, EFP capacity auctions disadvantage renewables, because they would be derated on their ability to provide reliable capacity. But this is exactly the point of the auctions. The derating simply takes into account the costs of variability, which have to be borne at a system level by calling forth extra capacity from, for instance, peaking plants.

Furthermore, this fact should have some interesting consequences for the renewables sector. Suddenly, renewables would be faced with an incentive – firm up supply, or be derated by the EFP auction. How might a renewable generating company react? They might decide to take the derating on the chin, and accept their electricity is less valuable to the grid than that provided by, say, a nuclear power station. Alternatively, they might invest in batteries (and devote resources towards further R&D into energy storage). They might cut side-deals with other generators to ramp up supply when they cannot. They might even negotiate with power-hungry consumers who can turn down their power usage during times of variability, such as certain industrial works, thus reducing overall demand on the grid.

This incentive, perhaps more than anything else, would provide a market stimulus for the advancement of energy storage and demand-shifting technologies, and help firm up renewables to the point where they can occupy larger shares of Britain's total energy needs without compromising security of supply.

Transitioning towards single EFP capacity auctions would signal a significant change in the way energy works in Britain. But, as Helm notes, EFP is 'not a radically new concept', and is already utilised by Ofgem and the National Grid.[196]

Certainly, the adoption of single EFP capacity auctions would not, and could not,

---

196 Ibid.

be an overnight decision. But it is perfectly possible for this Government to at least set the wheels in motion.

In return, Britain would gain an energy system in which renewables are normalised, security of supply is maintained, and the worst vestiges of regulations and subsidies and lobbying which plague the current approach are cast aside. The intellectual framework for single EFP capacity auctions already exists. It now requires a committed government to put it into practice.

5) Facilitate the next generation of reactor designs.

The UK was home to the first full-scale civil nuclear power station.[197] Since Calder Hall generated its first spark in 1956, it and the subsequent nuclear reactors which followed have consistently delivered a baseload amount of reliable, zero-carbon power. Had the electricity they generated come from coal-fired power stations, or even fossil gas, millions of additional tonnes of greenhouse gases and air pollutants would have been released into the atmosphere. Nuclear power has slowed the rate of climate change – and this Government should not shy away from the contribution it has made, and can still make, to achieving a cleaner energy system.

To ensure that the nuclear industry can play a starring role in the bid to decarbonise power in line with Net Zero – as well as providing other services, such as decarbonised heat and green hydrogen production – the Government should reappraise the regulatory landscape specific to the nuclear industry.

In particular, it must consider how the next generation of nuclear technologies will slot into the future energy system. While the history of nuclear power stations has typically been to develop ever larger reactor capacities, many now predict a reversal of this trend – with developers instead opting to construct SMRs, which can in theory be built more quickly,[198] at a lower cost, and fulfil different purposes in the energy system (such as load following as opposed to strict baseload generation).[199]

> **The intellectual framework for single EFP capacity auctions already exists. It now requires a committed government to put it into practice.**

Given how different such reactors will be, it is incumbent on the UK to ensure it has an adequately responsive regulatory framework, which accommodates SMRs and advanced reactors. While we are not in any way calling for a watering down of the health and safety regulations which are so obviously required for any nuclear technology, it is perfectly reasonable for the Government to consult with industry and regulators to identify what could be improved upon to get future nuclear projects from the drawing board to physical infrastructure in as short a time as necessary, at as low a cost as possible.

As should be the case with all regulation, a good regulatory landscape is one which is adaptive to innovation within industries

---

197 Institution of Civil Engineers, *Calder Hall nuclear power station.* Link.

198 None are as yet commercialised.

199 Michael Liebreich, *We Need To Talk About Nuclear Power.* Link.

– and, in fact, failure to keep up with such developments arguably undermines the supposed ends of regulations to begin with.

The Government should not stop at simply reviewing British regulations, however. One of the novel benefits of SMRs relative to larger reactors is that they could well become an exportable product – and one which the UK could lead in providing. To maximise the extent to which this is possible, some degree of international regulatory harmonisation is probably necessary.

> **❝ One of the novel benefits of SMRs relative to larger reactors is that they could well become an exportable product – and one which the UK could lead in providing.❞**

Already, work has been undertaken by the nuclear industry itself to investigate the possibility of facilitating some form of international licensing regime for SMRs.[200] Pushing this agenda further could be critical to driving down the costs of SMRs, as economic friction is reduced if an SMR developer knows its design can be sold in a multitude of countries – instead of having to produce bespoke designs for each country it wishes to sell to. With the UK hosting the COP26 climate conference in November this year, this could be a perfect time to hasten this agenda.[201]

It goes without saying that because of their smaller size, if SMRs are to plug gaps left by the decommissioning of existing, large-

scale nuclear power stations, many more of them will be required. Encouragingly, analysis from the Energy Technologies Institute – while heavily caveated – argues that there is considerable scope to add SMR capacity on existing nuclear sites across England and Wales.[202]

But if SMRs are to attract the R&D investment necessary to seriously compete in the energy system, longer-term thinking about where they will be sited is required. As such, the Government should draw up an extensive list of new sites for SMR development. Doing so would provide certainty to the industry that there will be a place for their product to eventually involve itself in Britain's future energy system. It would also ensure that as many possible players in the nuclear industry could enter the SMR market, knowing that there will be sites primed for development, and thus allow for market competition to take off.

All new nuclear power stations encounter considerable opposition – and this will be true of SMRs in particular, as they will likely be located closer to industrial clusters or residential areas than existing power stations. The Government should of course be sympathetic to local residents' concerns – but it should not capitulate entirely at the first sign of resistance.

With all types of new development, there is a tendency to think that the opposition outweighs the support, because the former generally tend to be better organised. Yet opinion polling around the favourability of nuclear power stations often shows that those located nearest to developments actually tend to be more supportive than the wider public.[203,204] They can see first-

---

200 World Nuclear Association, *Facilitating International Licensing of Small Modular Reactors*. Link.

201 Suffice to say, harmonising international regulations on conventional-scale nuclear, too, would be a laudable objective.

202 Energy Technologies Institute, *Nuclear: The role for nuclear within a ow carbon energy system*. Link.

203 Private data.

204 Matt Rooney, *Small Modular Reactors: The next big thing in energy?* Link.

hand the economic benefits which the sites bring to the local areas, and probably have a better understanding of nuclear energy than the projects' detractors.

In determining where new nuclear developments might be sited, therefore, the Government ought to consider local feelings, but not to give them excessive weight. In all likelihood, that opposition will give way to net support in years to come – as well as the well-paying jobs, energy security, and all the rest.

If Britain is to have a successful nuclear industry in the future, it is crucial that the Government provides the conditions necessary for it to flourish. This does not mean granting it preferential favours, and certainly does not mean any sort of reduction in regulations which protect the public and the environment. But small tweaks to the regulatory landscape, which ensure it is fit for purpose and responsive to sector developments, could make all the difference in terms of fostering a prosperous nuclear industry.

VI. Conclusion

At the heart of the UK's economic prosperity is an intricate energy system which ensures individuals and businesses have access to a reliable stream of energy where they need it, when they need it.

Few things are more important than guaranteeing that this energy system remains robust.

But this is not to say that the building blocks of Britain's energy system must remain the same as they have always been. On the contrary, it is critical that zero-carbon energy generation methods continue to replace ones which are fossil-fuelled. Failure to do so will write off any realistic hope of the country reaching its 2030 and 2050 climate objectives.

Here, the Government has a crucial role to play. As we have discussed in this report, it has the ability to make sure that the requisite policy frameworks are in place to allow the transition to a cleaner, smarter future energy system – in such a way that is economically prudent, in line with climate science, and does not risk energy insecurity.

Given the time scales at which the energy industry moves, it would be conceited to think that anyone can accurately predict

exactly how the sector will look like in 30 years' time. But in the nearer term, some things are certain. Electrification of the economy will increase – with the power facilitating this change coming ever more from zero-emission sources such as onshore and offshore wind turbines, solar PV, and nuclear reactors. Improvements in energy storage, in the form of batteries and green hydrogen, plus demand-side response and other technologies, will certainly help mitigate some of renewables' perennial issues.

Recent developments have already rendered coal-fired power generation redundant, and will steadily do the same for fossil gas. Yet while renewables will surely make further inroads, it is not clear whether they will be able to supplant fossil-fuelled generation entirely – as will be required for the UK to hit Net Zero by 2050.

> **❝ Given the time scales at which the energy industry moves, it would be conceited to think that anyone can accurately predict exactly how the sector will look like in 30 years' time. ❞**

All the while, the UK is due to retire almost all of its nuclear reactors over the course of the coming decade – thus losing a critical amount of reliable, zero-emission power.

Failure to replace this baseload capacity in a timely fashion risks the UK defaulting on its climate goals, as well as the security of the energy supply.

Therefore, we argue that the UK must commit to keeping its nuclear industry going, at least in the near-term. The Government should be a champion of nuclear power, and recognise the potential it has to help deliver on its climate objectives and provide many other benefits.

> **❝ An additional nuclear site would provide a guarantee of dependable zero-emission energy, able to keep the lights on when renewables cannot.❞**

For now, this should mean supporting the construction of one more nuclear power station by delivering a financing model which works for all parties concerned – most probably the RAB model, but with tight cost controls on an ex ante basis.

An additional nuclear site would provide a guarantee of dependable zero-emission energy, able to keep the lights on when renewables cannot. It would also act as a bridge, giving Britain the breathing space to develop, refine, and install the generating and storage technologies of tomorrow.

Importantly, it would retain the pipeline of skills and jobs in the industry, located across the length and breadth of the country, too. Having this in place will be vital if the UK is to seamlessly transition to constructing next generation nuclear technologies – such as SMRs and fusion reactors – if such technologies are able to mature in time and be competitive with renewables plus storage.

For too long, Britain's energy system has been plagued by indecision, and a lack of forward thinking. The consequences of this are showing up in sharp relief today. The Government has mapped out a bold, big-picture vision for how the energy will work in the future. But it needs to start the process of making that a reality, while dealing with its most pressing problem – ensuring there is security of emissions-free supply which can keep the lights on without further heating up the planet.

As should be clear from the past few years, inaction simply stores up problems for later generations – something which makes neither economic, environmental, nor ethical sense. Instead, the Government can lay the foundations for a radically cleverer, cleaner, cheaper energy system – a legacy which any administration should be proud of leaving.

Bibliography

Adam Thierer, *Permissionless Innovation: The Continuing Case for Comprehensive Technological Freedom.*

Amy Mount and Dustin Benton, *Getting more from less realising the potential of negawatts in the UK electricity market.*

Anil Markandya and Paul Wilkinson, *Electricity generation and health.*

Anna Holligan, *Jet fuel from thin air: Aviation's hope or hype?*

BBC News, *Moorside: Nuclear power schemes proposed for Cumbria site.*

Benjamin Sovacool et al., *Balancing safety with sustainability: assessing the risk of accidents for modern low-carbon energy systems.*

Cambridge Economic Policy Associates, *Background evidence: Review of the UK infrastructure financing market.*

Carbon Tax Centre, *Cap and trade.*

Carsten Jung and Luke Murphy, *Transforming the economy after COVID-19: A clean, fair and resilient recovery.*

Citizens Advice, *Response to BEIS consultation on adopting a RAB model for new nuclear projects.*

Citizens' Climate Lobby, *Household Impact Study: Financial Impact on Households of Carbon Fee and Dividend.*

Climate Assembly UK, *The path to net zero: Climate Assembly UK: Full report.*

Climate Change Committee, *The Sixth Carbon Budget: The UK's Path to Net Zero.*

Climate Change Committee, *Sixth Carbon Budget – Dataset.*

Committee on Climate Change, *Net Zero Technical report.*

Committee on Climate Change, *Net Zero: The UK's contribution to stopping global warming.*

Committee on Climate Change, *Reducing UK emissions: 2019 Progress Report to Parliament.*

Conservative and Unionist Party, *Get Brexit Done: Unleash Britain's Potential.*

Department for Business, Energy and Industrial Strategy and the Prime Minister's Office, 10 Downing Street, *UK sets ambitious new climate target ahead of UN Summit.*

Department for Business, Energy and Industrial Strategy and the Prime Minister's Office, 10 Downing Street, *UK sets ambitious new climate target ahead of UN Summit.*

Department for Business, Energy and Industrial Strategy, *2019 UK greenhouse gas emissions, provisional figures.*

Department for Business, Energy and Industrial Strategy, *BEIS 2018 Updated Energy & Emissions Projections.*

Department for Business, Energy and Industrial Strategy, *Contracts for Difference.*

Department for Business, Energy and Industrial Strategy, *Digest of United Kingdom Energy Statistics 2020.*

Department for Business, Energy and Industrial Strategy, *Early phase out of unabated coal generation in Great Britain.*

Department for Business, Energy and Industrial Strategy, *Electricity Generation Costs 2020.*

Department for Business, Energy and Industrial Strategy, *Energy Trends: UK electricity: Fuel Used in electricity generation and electricity supplied (ET 5.1 – quarterly).*

Department for Business, Energy and Industrial Strategy, *Energy and emissions projections.*

Department for Business, Energy and Industrial Strategy, *Energy Trends March 2019.*

Department for Business, Energy and Industrial Strategy, *Final UK greenhouse gas emissions national statistics: 1990 to 2018.*

Department for Business, Energy and Industrial Strategy, *Fuel used in electricity generation and electricity supplied.*

Department for Business, Energy and Industrial Strategy, *Hinkley Point C.*

Department for Business, Energy and Industrial Strategy, *Historical electricity data: 1920 to 2019.*

Department for Business, Energy and Industrial Strategy, *Participating in the UK ETS.*

Department for Business, Energy and Industrial Strategy, *RAB model for Nuclear: Consultation on a RAB model for new nuclear projects.*

Department for Business, Energy and Industrial Strategy, *RAB model for Nuclear: Government response to the consultation on a RAB model for new nuclear projects.*

Department for Business, Energy and Industrial Strategy, *UK becomes first major economy to pass net zero emissions law.*

Department for Business, Energy and Industrial Strategy, *UK Research and Development Roadmap.*

Department for Digital, Media, Culture and Sport and the National Cyber Security Centre, *Huawei to be removed from UK 5G networks by 2027.*

Department of Energy and Climate Change, *National Policy Statement for Nuclear Power Generation (EN-6): Volume I of II.*

Dieter Helm, *Cost of Energy Review.*

Eamonn Butler, *Public Choice – A primer.*

Eamonn Ives, *Driving Change: How Hydrogen Can Fuel a Transport Revolution.*

Eamonn Ives, *Green Entrepreneurship.*

Eamonn Ives, *Nuclear reactors: is big beautiful?*

Eamonn Ives, *We need a carbon border tax to get Britain to net zero.*

EDF and CGN, *Bradwell B.*

EDF, *Sizewell B power station.*

Energy and Climate Intelligence Unit, *Net zero: the scorecard.*

Energy Systems Catapult, *Decarbonisation of Heat: Why It Needs Innovation.*

Energy Systems Catapult, *Innovating to Net Zero: UK Net Zero Report.*

Energy Systems Catapult, *Nuclear for Net Zero.*

Energy Technologies Institute, *Nuclear: The role for nuclear within a ow carbon energy system.*

Energy Technologies Institute, *The ETI Nuclear Cost Drivers Project: Summary Report.*

Guy Stewart Callendar, *The artificial production of carbon dioxide and its influence on temperature.*

Hannah Ritchie and Max Roser, CO_2 *and Greenhouse Gas Emissions.*

Henry Fountain, *Compact Nuclear Fusion Reactor Is 'Very Likely to Work,' Studies Suggest.*

HM Government, *Meeting the Energy Challenge: A White Paper on Nuclear Power.*

HM Government, *Powering our Net Zero Future.*

HM Government, *The Energy Challenge.*

HM Government, *The Ten Point Plan for a Green Industrial Revolution: Building back better, supporting green jobs, and accelerating our path to net zero. Link.*

HM Treasury, *Budget 2020. Link.*

HM Treasury, *Response to the National Infrastructure Assessment.*

House of Commons Hansard, *Nuclear power: 04 June 2018: Volume 642.*

House of Commons Library, *Carbon Price Floor (CPF) and price support mechanism.*

House of Commons Library, *New Nuclear Power.*

House of Commons Library, *Support for low carbon power.*

Iain McDowell, *RHI Inquiry: Cash-for-ash – the story so far.*

Ian Preston, Joshua Thumin et al., *Distribution of carbon emissions in the UK: Implications for domestic energy policy.*

Institution of Civil Engineers, *Calder Hall nuclear power station.*

Intergovernmental Panel on Climate Change, *Global warming of 1.5°C: An IPCC Special Report on the impacts of global warming of 1.5°C above pre-industrial levels and related global greenhouse gas emission pathways, in the context of strengthening the global response to the threat of climate change, sustainable development, and efforts to eradicate poverty.*

International Energy Agency, *Nuclear Power in a Clean Energy System.*

International Energy Association, *Direct Air Capture.*

International Renewable Energy Agency, *Renewable Power Generation Costs in 2019.*

International Renewable Energy Agency, *Utility-scale batteries.*

Jillian Ambrose, *Government to rethink Hinkley Point funding model for future projects.*

Jim Pickard and David Sheppard, *Hitachi preparing to pull out of nuclear project in blow to UK climate ambitions.*

Kirsty Gogan and Eric Ingersoll, *Drivers of Cost and Risk in Nuclear New Build Reflecting International Experience.*

Kristian Niemietz, *Redefining the Poverty Debate.*

Mark Pennington, *Liberty, Markets, and Environmental Values: A Hayekian Defense of Free-Market Environmentalism.*

Martin Roeb, Christos Agrafiotis and Christian Sattler, *Hydrogen production via thermochemical water splitting.*

Matt Rooney, *Small Modular Reactors: The next big thing in energy?*

Michael Liebreich, *We Need To Talk About Nuclear Power.*

NASA, *Carbon Dioxide.*

National Audit Office, *Hinkley Point C.*

National Grid ESO, *Future Energy Scenarios: July 2020.*

National Grid ESO, *How smart charging can help unlock flexible capacity from EVs.*

National Infrastructure Commission, *Net Zero: Opportunities for the power sector.*

Nuclear Decommissioning Authority, *Radioactive Waste Industry 2019 UK data.*

Nuclear Industry Association, *BEIS consultation: Regulated Asset Base model for nuclear.*

Nuclear Industry Association, *Nuclear Generation.*

Ørsted, *Hornsea Two: Powering well over 1.3 million homes with green electricity.*

Paul Denholm et al., *Intertia and the Power Grid: A Guide Without the Spin.*

Prime Minister's Office, 10 Downing Street and the Department for Business, Energy and Industrial Strategy, *New plans to make UK world leader in green energy.*

Prime Minister's Office, 10 Downing Street, the Department for Business, Energy and Industrial Strategy and the Department for International Development, *British scientists to help tackle climate change through new £1 billion fund.*

PwC, *The Low Carbon Economy Index 2019.*

RenewableUK, *Powering the Future: RenewableUK's Vision of the Transition.*

Richard Howard, *Next steps for the Carbon Price Floor.*

Robert Colvile, *Popular Capitalism.*

Robert D. Marchand, S.C. Lenny Koh and Jonathan C. Morris, *Delivering energy efficiency and carbon reduction schemes in England: Lessons from Green Deal Pioneer Places.*

Royal Society, *Nuclear cogeneration: civil nuclear energy in a low-carbon future.*

Sam Bowman and Eleanor Mack, *Open Energy: Using data to create a smarter, cheaper and fairer energy market.*

Sam Bowman and Stian Westlake, *Reviving Economic Thinking on the Right: A short plan for the UK.*

Sam Lowe, *Should the UK introduce a border carbon adjustment mechanism?*

Shripad T. Revankar, *Nuclear Hydrogen Production.*

Simon Evans, *Record-low price for UK offshore wind cheaper than existing gas plants by 2023.*

Simon Evans, *The Swiss company hoping to capture 1% of global CO_2 emissions by 2025.*

Simon Evans, *The UK becomes first major economy to set net-zero climate goal.*

The Economist, *Climate policy needs negative carbon-dioxide emissions.*

Tony Blair, *Speech at the CBI annual dinner (16 May 2006).*

Tony Lodge, *The Great Carbon Swindle: How the UK hides its emissions abroad.*

Toshiba Corporation, *Toshiba to Take Steps to Wind-up NuGeneration, Withdraw from Nuclear Power Plant Construction Project in UK, and to Record of Loss on Valuation of Stocks of Subsidiaries and Affiliates (Non-consolidated).*

UK Energy Research Centre, *Funding a Low Carbon Energy System: a fairer approach?*

UK Parliament, *Hinkley Point C Power Station: Question for Department for Business, Energy and Industrial Strategy: UIN HL2607, tabled on 26 October 2017.*

Umwelt Bundesamt, *Indicator: Greenhouse gas emissions.*

United States Environmental Protection Agency, *Greenhouse Gas Inventory Data Explorer.*

Valeria Perasso, *Turning carbon dioxide into rock – forever.*

World Bank, *GDP (current US$) – United Kingdom.*

World Bank, *Population, total – United Kingdom.*

World Nuclear Association, *Facilitating International Licensing of Small Modular Reactors.*

World Nuclear Association, *Financing Nuclear Energy.*

World Nuclear News, *New nuclear for Sellafield.*

Jonathan Ford, *US consortium revives plan for Welsh nuclear power plant.*